Encyclopedia of 312
Scroll Saw Designs

by John La Forge

About the Author

John La Forge was born at home in the small town of Woodson, Texas (pop. 354). He grew up in Breckenridge, a west-central Texas oil town, where his father practiced veterinary medicine.

La Forge took an early interest in wood crafting and has followed it as a hobby since about age eight.

Although educated as a band director at North Texas State University, La Forge pursued a career in public relations and publishing until establishing La Forge Music Company.

La Forge and his wife Patricia are the parents of a son and two daughters.

Acknowledgements

This book would not have been possible without the patience and understanding of my wife, Patricia, and my family. Nor would this book have been possible without the support and prayers of a true master craftsman. L. D. Baxley has shared his time, his patterns and his considerable expertise with me over the years as well as being a fantastic friend and neighbor, regardless of the miles that have separated us.

Table of Contents

How to Use This Book

The modern scroll saw has enabled the craftsman to plunge headlong into a new and exciting era of handwork. Intricate designs are now completed in minutes rather than in the hours that used to be necessary.

The following patterns represent the most popular designs seen at countless fairs and flea markets. These patterns are designed to utilize common stock readily available. Pine is the most used material, although 1/8, 3/16 and 1/4 inch cabinet grade laminate is also a favorite material for many items, especially for small items that are used to decorate larger objects. Thin laminate is also recommended for magnet backed "refrigerator" items.

Shelves can be joined with a good quality wood glue and finishing nails. Intricate joining techniques are not used for simplicity and to maintain a rustic country look.

Knots are generally left in place, although a soft wood filler is applied over the knots, as well as in nail holes prior to sanding.

A more finished look is achieved by routing the front edges and the inside cuts with a 1/4 inch round-over bit with a 1/4 inch pilot. The pilot type bit is not necessary, but it will help prevent router burns. HSS (high speed steel) bits can be used on pine, although carbide tipped bits will last much longer.

A drill press or drill stand is preferred on pieces with pegs in order to achieve better spacing and truer alignment of the pegs. The drill press or drill stand is easier to use when drilling holes to hang the objects.

If a drill press or drill stand is not available, you can make a simple angle guide by sawing a 1x1 or 1x2 at the desired angle. Align the angled cut with the spot you want to drill and clamp the guide in place. Use the angle guide to drill the hole (see illustration).

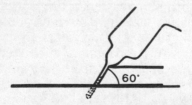

Enlarging, Transferring and Finishing Patterns

Sizing a project to meet your needs is very simple. You may use any of three methods to enlarge or reduce patterns.

The first and, by far, the easiest method is to have the pattern xerographically enlarged or reduced. This can be done with a copy

7

machine that has reduction and enlargement capabilities. If the copy machine can only enlarge to double the size of the original, you can enlarge the enlargement to reach the desired size.

The second method is to determine the ratio of the pattern to the size you want. The grid used in this book is 1/2 inch square. If you want a finished project to be twice the size of the pattern, lay down grid lines that are one inch square. If you want the item to be three times the size shown, make your grid 1-1/2 inches square.

Determine where the pattern lines cross each grid line and mark your grid in the corresponding spot. This is done grid by grid. After putting a dot where the pattern line intersects each grid line, it's simply a process of connecting the dots with curved lines where necessary. Curved lines are simple to free-hand. Use a pencil to make your patterns so that if a correction is needed, it will be easy to do. Any pattern that is to be the same size can, of course, be traced onto opaque or transparent paper.

The third method of changing the size of a pattern is by using a pantograph. This simple machine's starting price is under ten dollars. The pantograph can enlarge up to ten times the original size and can reduce down to one-tenth of the original size.

The simplest method for transferring the pattern to the wood is to rubber cement the pattern directly onto the wood. But you destroy the pattern while cutting out the object, and you have to clean off the remaining rubber cement and paper.

The second method that is commonly used is to trace the pattern onto the wood using carbon paper.

Another method is to draw a grid on the wood and draw the pattern directly on the project. If the grid and pattern is drawn on very soft wood, sanding will be necessary to remove the indentations in the wood.

My favorite method is to transfer the original pattern to a template which is then cut out so that the pattern can be traced around the template onto the project. A template easily can be made from lightweight cardboard. If the pattern is to be used many times, the template can be made of thin laminate. Favorite patterns can be reproduced hundreds of times from a sturdy template.

For a finishing touch, brush acrylic (water base) paint onto the items chosen to be painted. Designs on the items are optional as are the colors of the items. A coat of clear acrylic sprayed on the painted items acts as a sealer and completes the project.

An Apple a Day

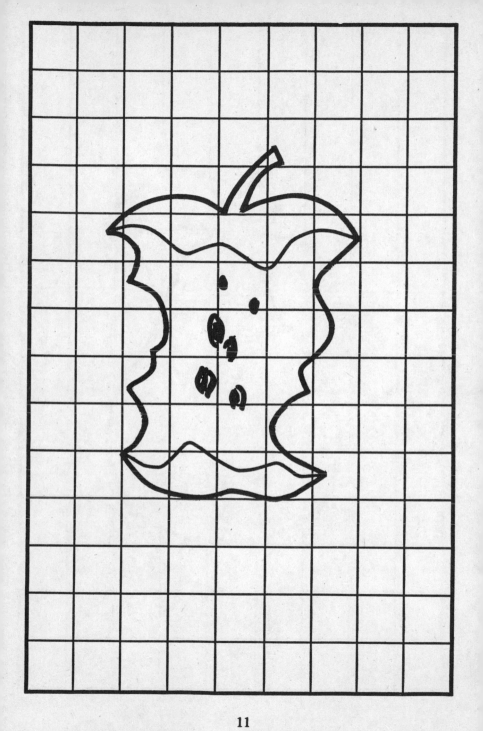

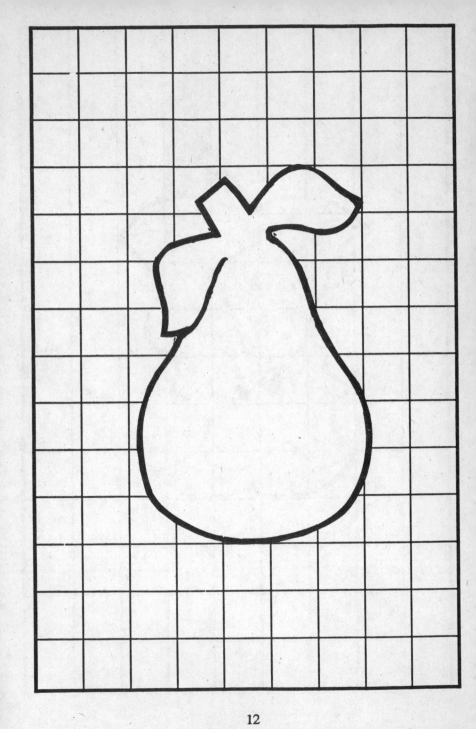

13

Wash Day

WASH DAY — Paint the kettle black. Use your choice of colors on the washerwoman's face, hands, dress, scarf and neckerchief. A small scrap of fabric draped from her hand to the kettle adds to the effect. Mount the woman and the kettle on a 1"x 4"x 8" length of board. Center the pieces.

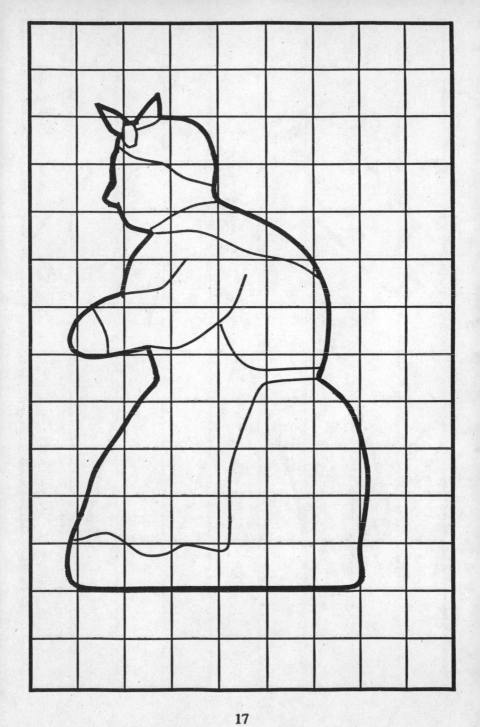

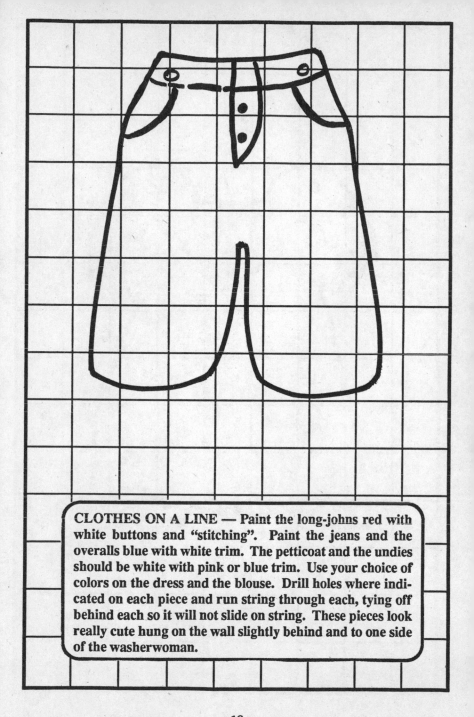

CLOTHES ON A LINE — Paint the long-johns red with white buttons and "stitching". Paint the jeans and the overalls blue with white trim. The petticoat and the undies should be white with pink or blue trim. Use your choice of colors on the dress and the blouse. Drill holes where indicated on each piece and run string through each, tying off behind each so it will not slide on string. These pieces look really cute hung on the wall slightly behind and to one side of the washerwoman.

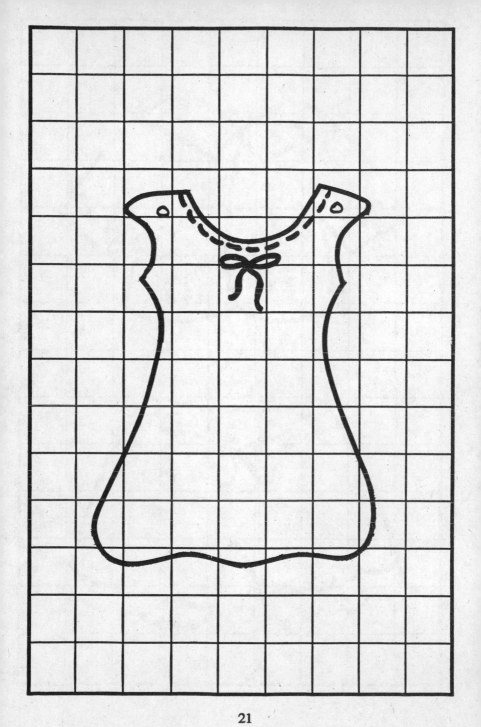

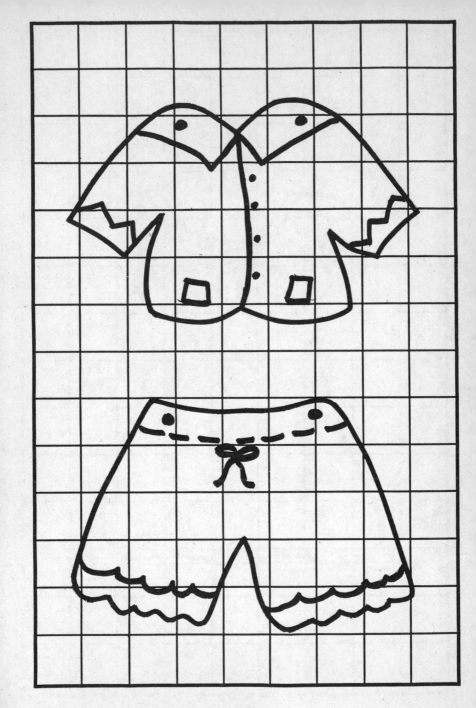

From the Heart

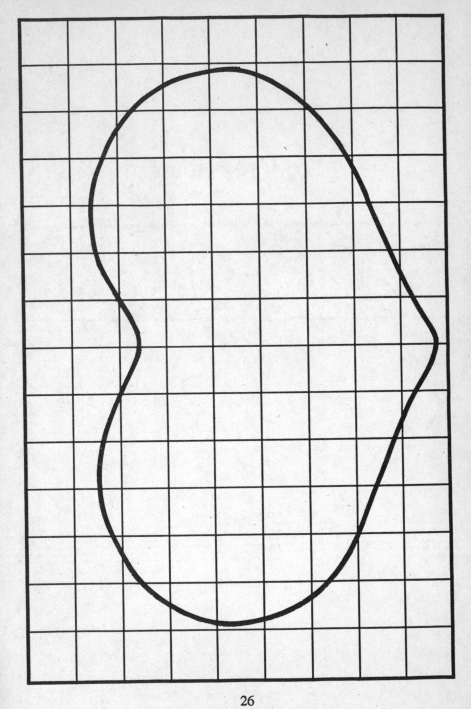

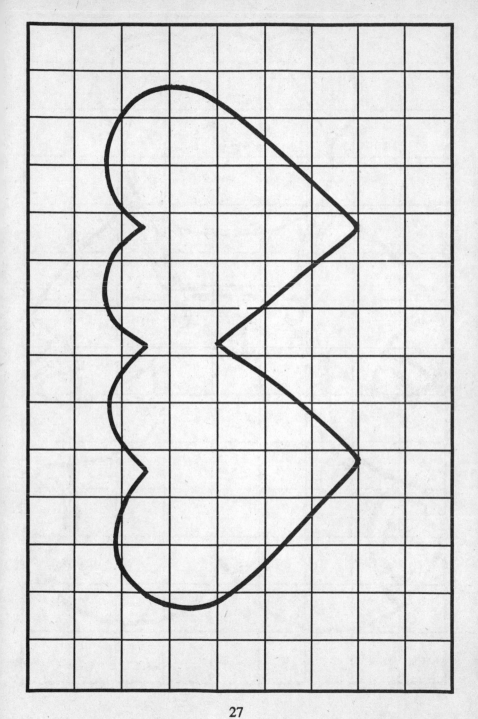

27

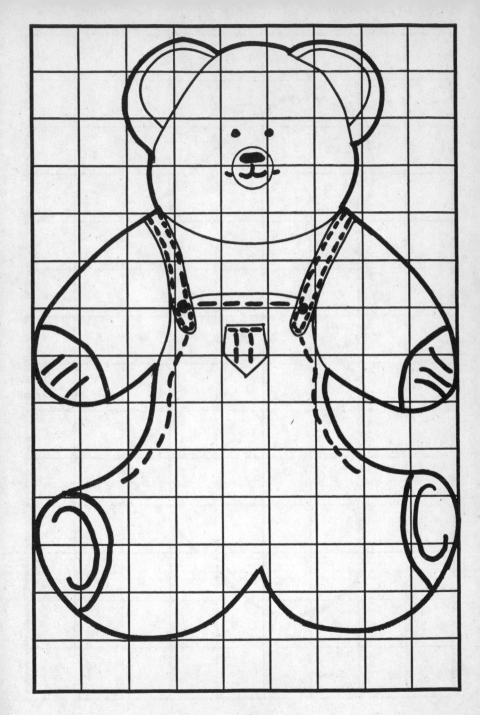

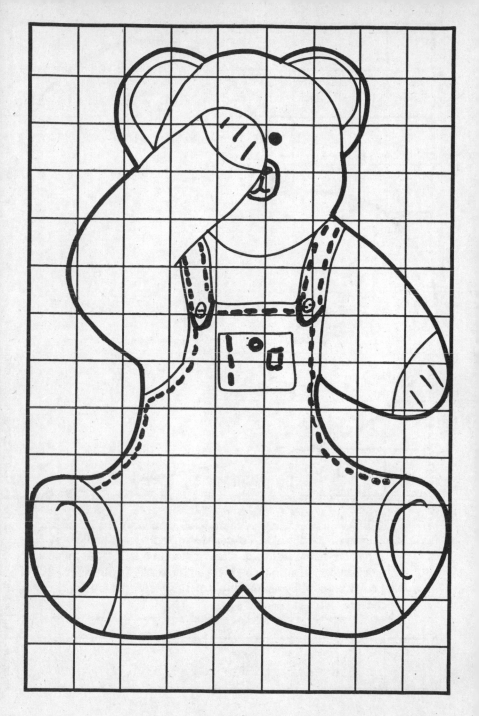

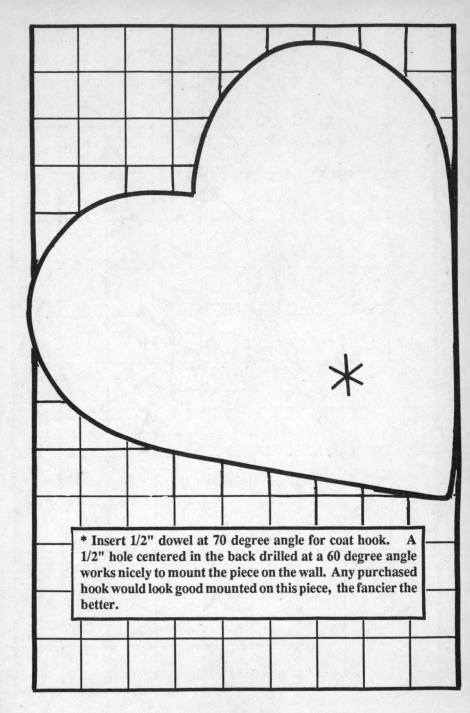

* Insert 1/2" dowel at 70 degree angle for coat hook. A 1/2" hole centered in the back drilled at a 60 degree angle works nicely to mount the piece on the wall. Any purchased hook would look good mounted on this piece, the fancier the better.

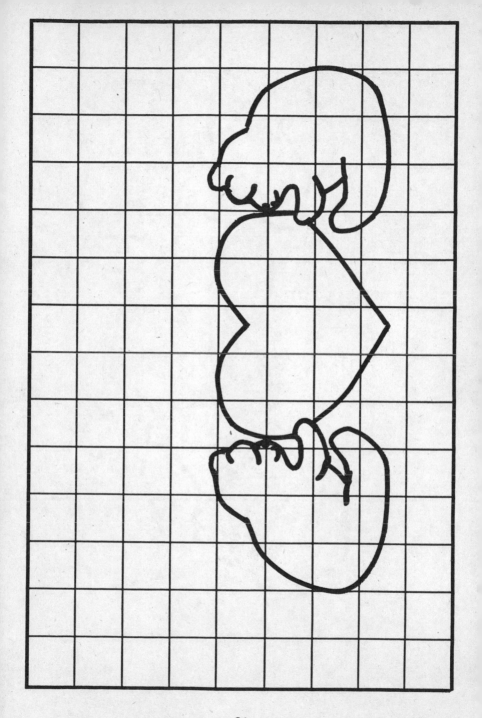

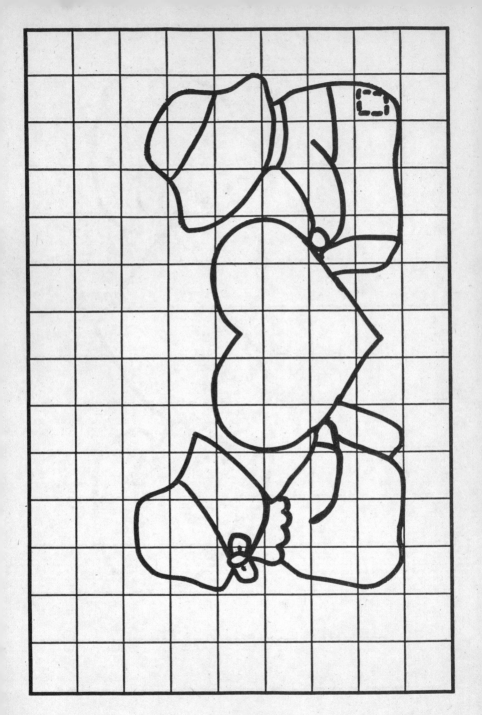

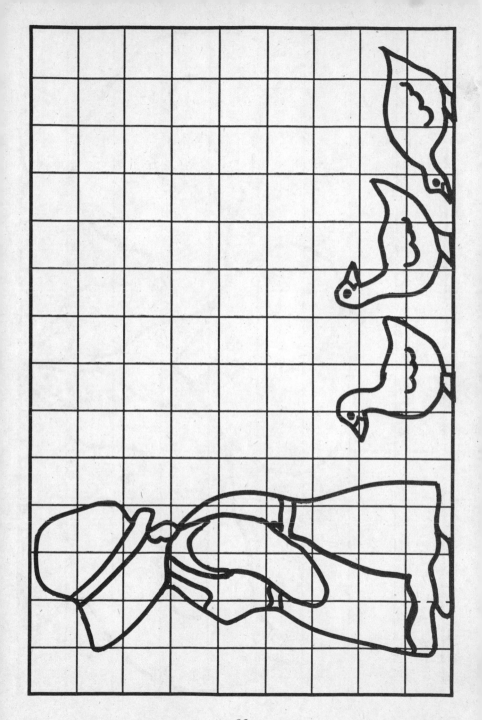

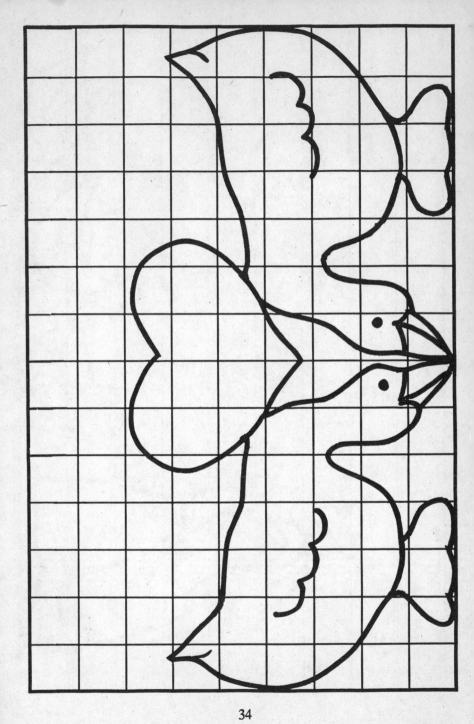

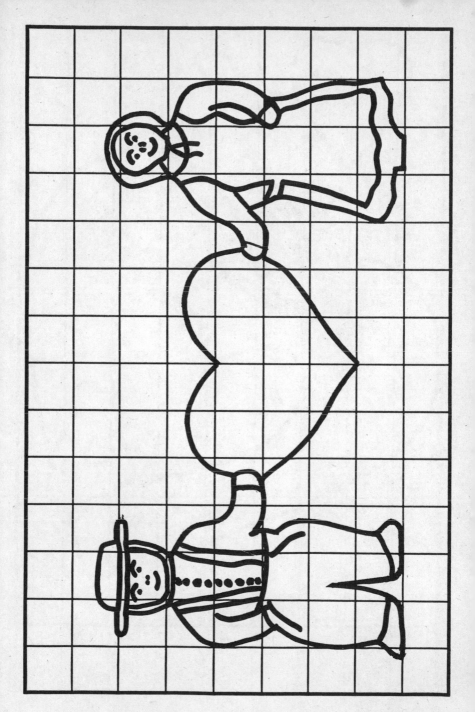

HANGING HEARTS — Glue hearts as shown. Hang with sisal bow.

Handy Around the House

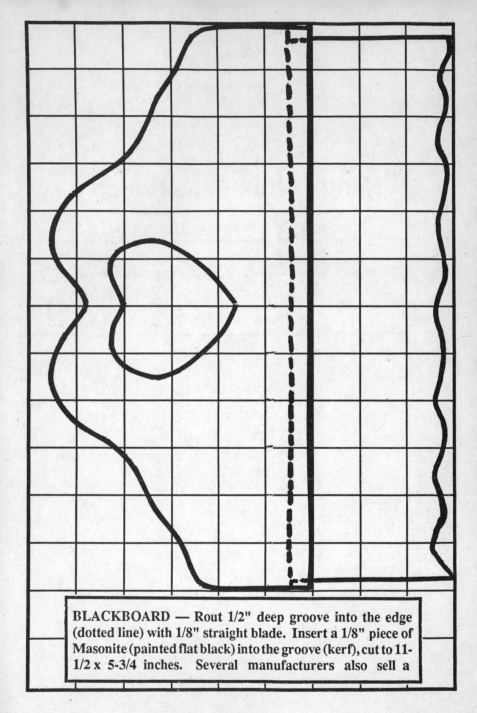

BLACKBOARD — Rout 1/2" deep groove into the edge (dotted line) with 1/8" straight blade. Insert a 1/8" piece of Masonite (painted flat black) into the groove (kerf), cut to 11-1/2 x 5-3/4 inches. Several manufacturers also sell a

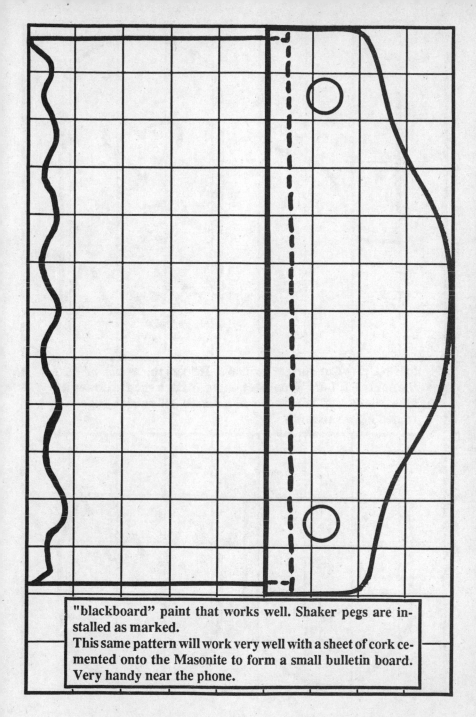

"blackboard" paint that works well. Shaker pegs are installed as marked.

This same pattern will work very well with a sheet of cork cemented onto the Masonite to form a small bulletin board. Very handy near the phone.

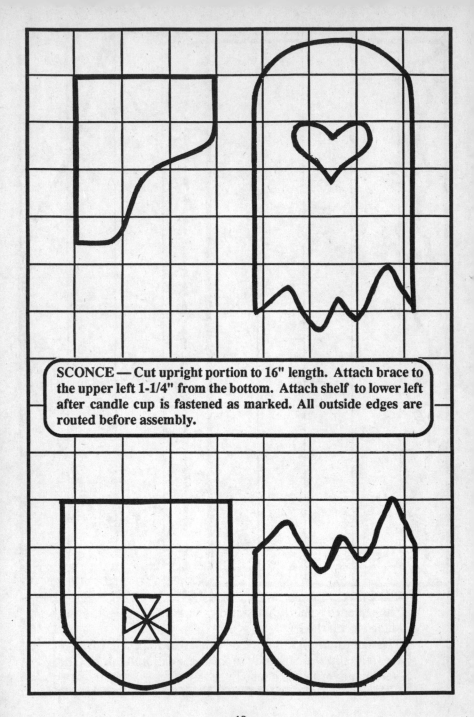

SCONCE — Cut upright portion to 16" length. Attach brace to the upper left 1-1/4" from the bottom. Attach shelf to lower left after candle cup is fastened as marked. All outside edges are routed before assembly.

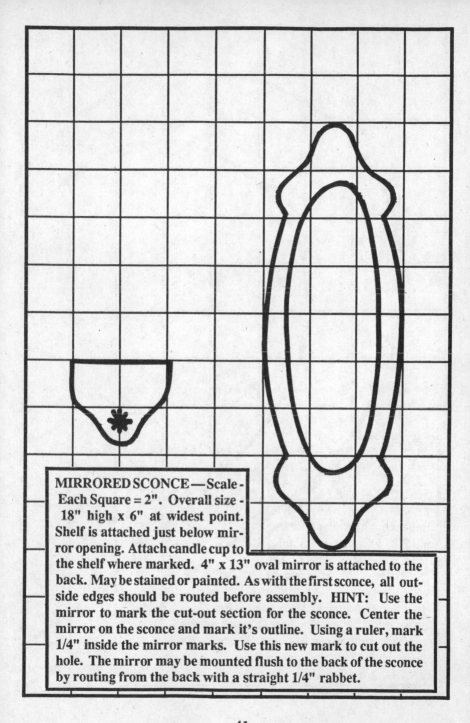

MIRRORED SCONCE — Scale - Each Square = 2". Overall size - 18" high x 6" at widest point. Shelf is attached just below mirror opening. Attach candle cup to the shelf where marked. 4" x 13" oval mirror is attached to the back. May be stained or painted. As with the first sconce, all outside edges should be routed before assembly. HINT: Use the mirror to mark the cut-out section for the sconce. Center the mirror on the sconce and mark it's outline. Using a ruler, mark 1/4" inside the mirror marks. Use this new mark to cut out the hole. The mirror may be mounted flush to the back of the sconce by routing from the back with a straight 1/4" rabbet.

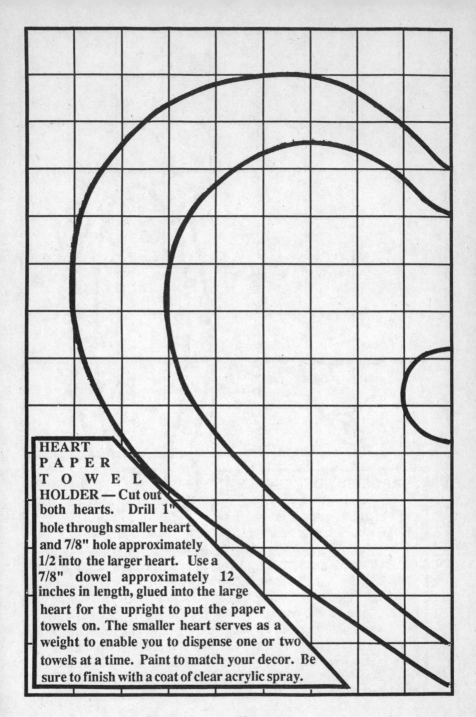

HEART PAPER TOWEL HOLDER — Cut out both hearts. Drill 1" hole through smaller heart and 7/8" hole approximately 1/2 into the larger heart. Use a 7/8" dowel approximately 12 inches in length, glued into the large heart for the upright to put the paper towels on. The smaller heart serves as a weight to enable you to dispense one or two towels at a time. Paint to match your decor. Be sure to finish with a coat of clear acrylic spray.

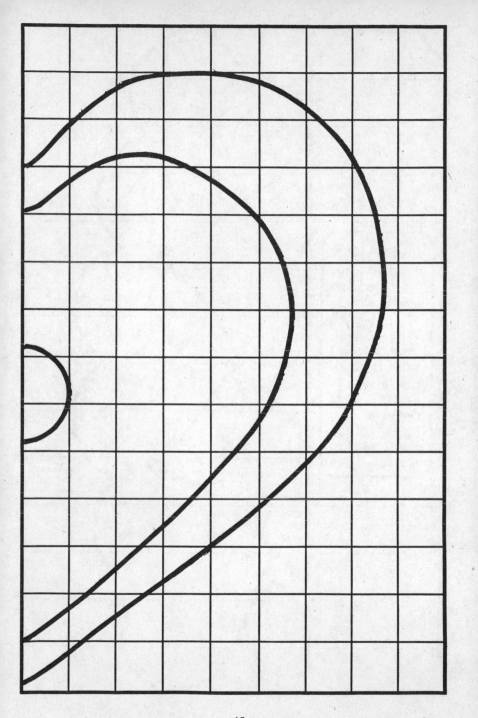

43

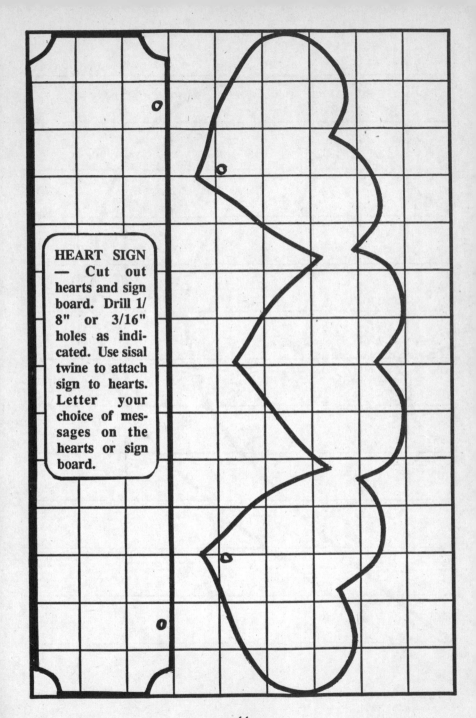

HEART SIGN — Cut out hearts and sign board. Drill 1/8" or 3/16" holes as indicated. Use sisal twine to attach sign to hearts. Letter your choice of messages on the hearts or sign board.

NOTE PAD — After cutting both pieces, drill 3/16" holes through both pieces as indicated. Tie with brightly colored gingham. Holds 4" x 6" note paper.

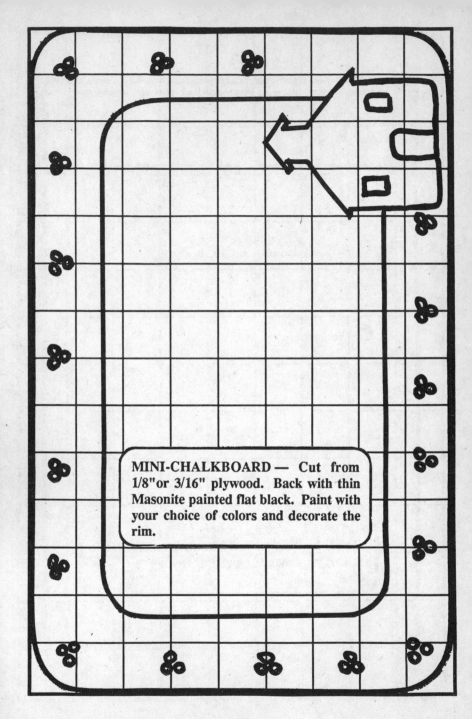

MINI-CHALKBOARD — Cut from 1/8"or 3/16" plywood. Back with thin Masonite painted flat black. Paint with your choice of colors and decorate the rim.

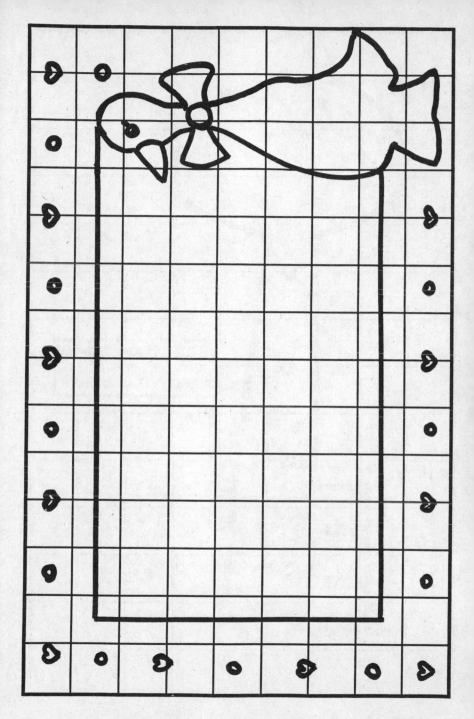

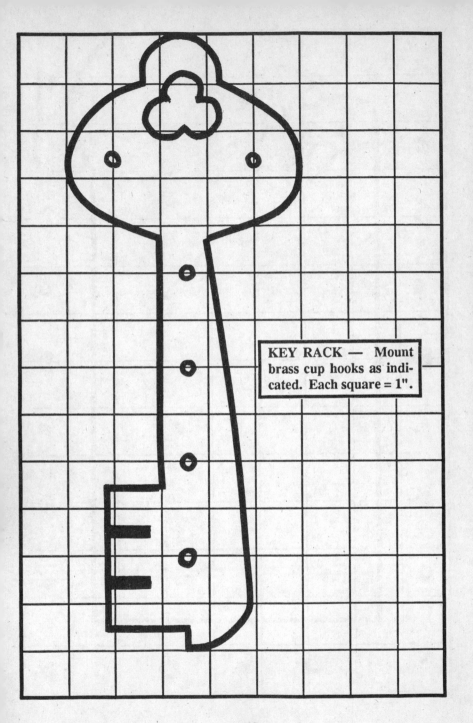

KEY RACK — Mount brass cup hooks as indicated. Each square = 1".

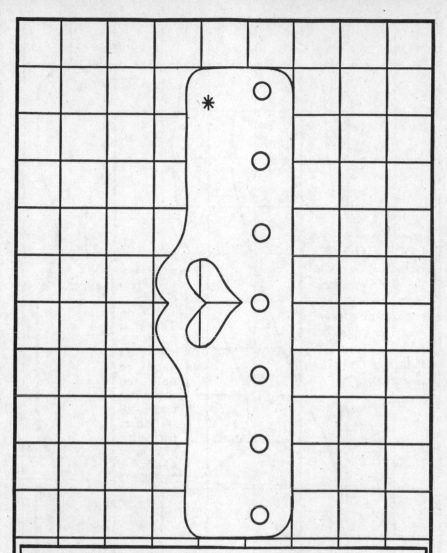

COUNTRY JEWELRY HOLDER — Cut from 1"x 4" stock. All front edges are routed with a 1/4" round-over bit with a 1/4" pilot. This can be done with a rasp. Seven small wheel hubs are utilized as pegs. Acrylic paint in your choice of colors followed by one coat of clear acrylic spray completes the piece. On the back of the piece, drill a 5/16" hole at a 70 degree angle 3/4" in from each outside edge as indicated (*) to hang piece.

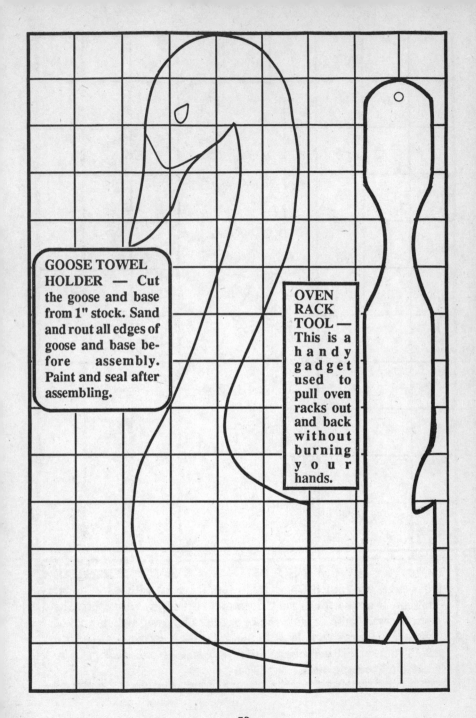

GOOSE TOWEL HOLDER — Cut the goose and base from 1" stock. Sand and rout all edges of goose and base before assembly. Paint and seal after assembling.

OVEN RACK TOOL — This is a handy gadget used to pull oven racks out and back without burning your hands.

50

BASE FOR GOOSE TOWEL HOLDER — Drill holes for Shaker pegs (3") as indicated. After sanding, attach base of goose's neck as shown with glue and finishing nails. Each square = 1".

Blue Yonder

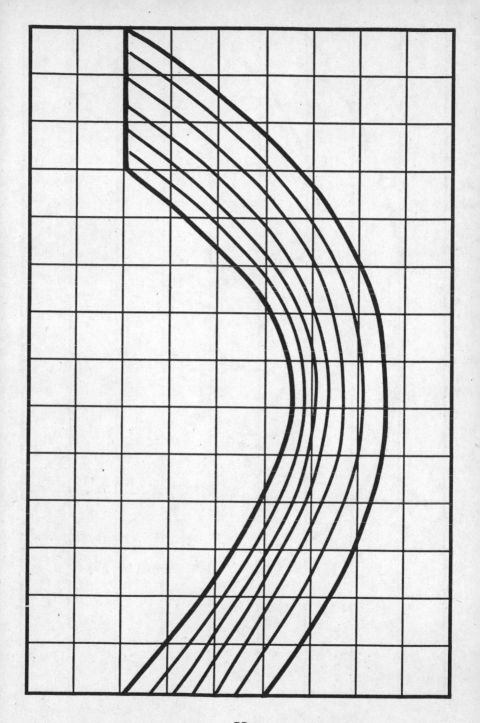

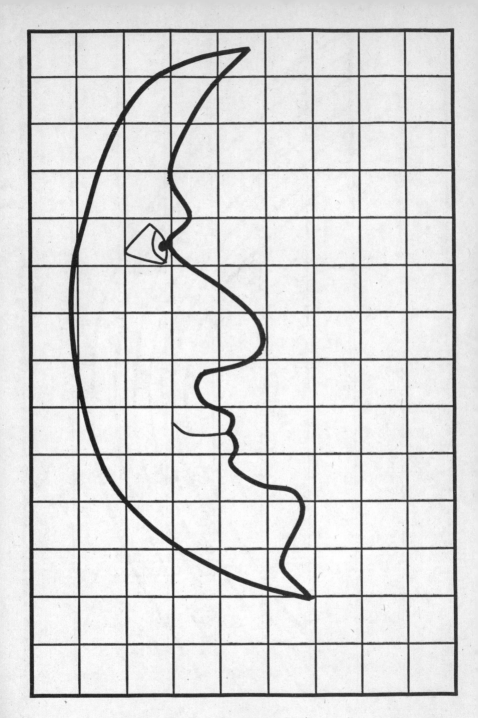

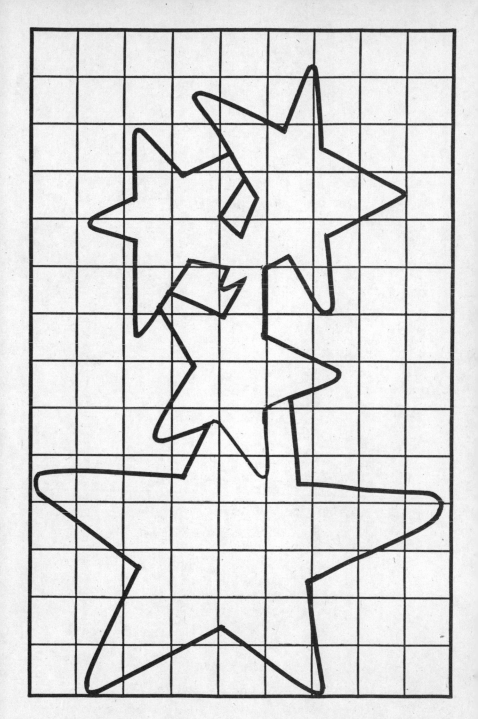

Down on the Farm

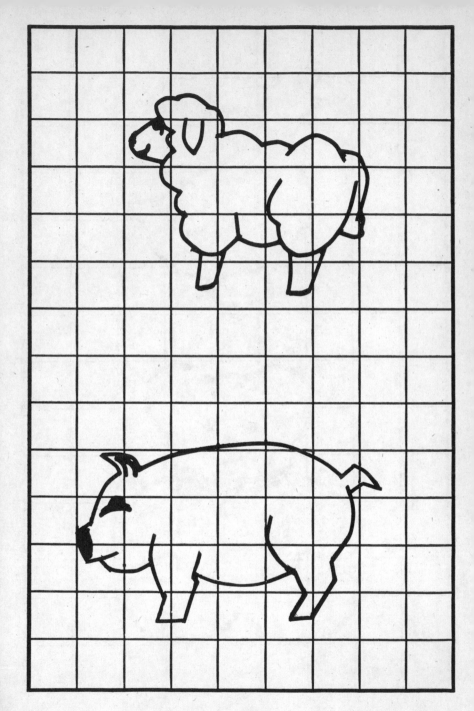

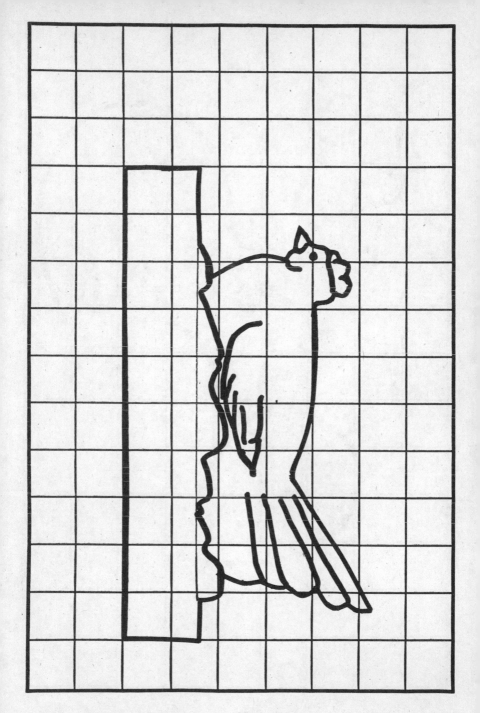

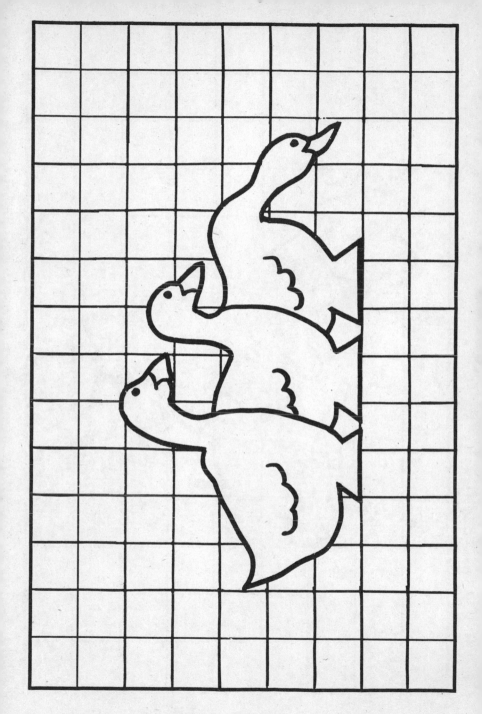

Across the Border

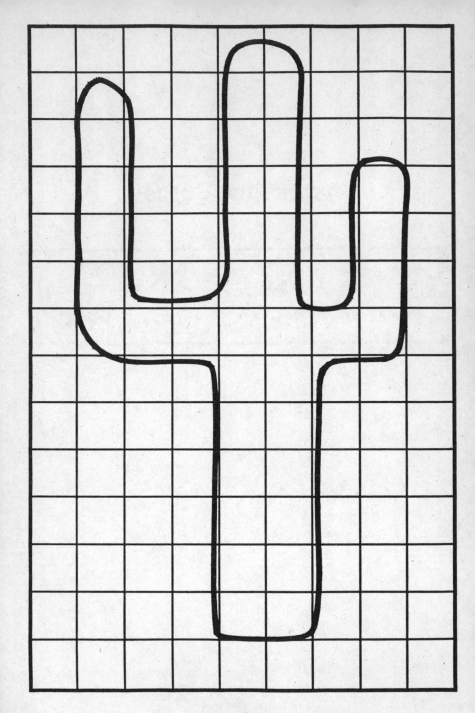

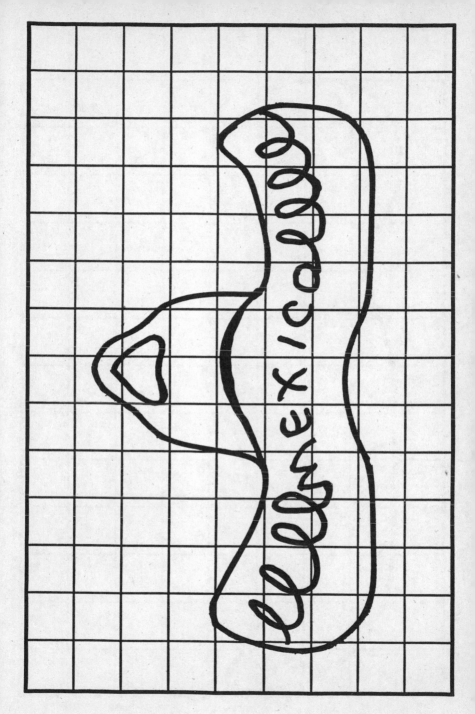

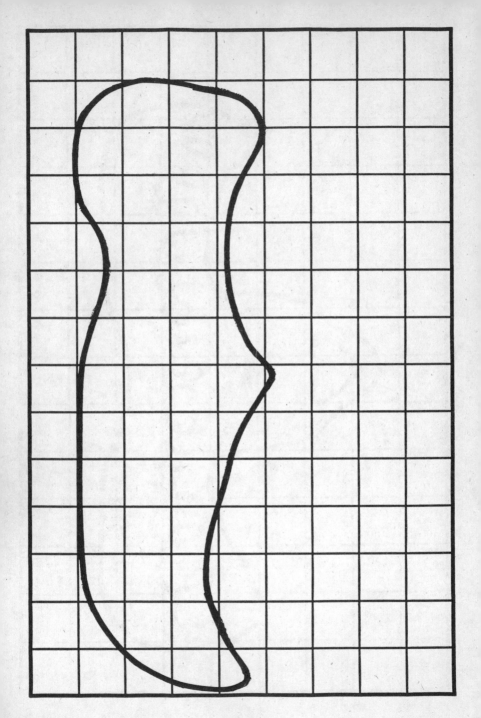

72

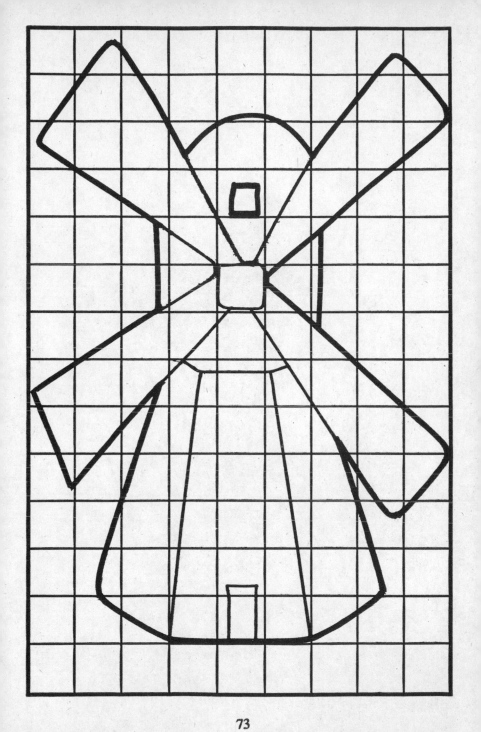

Critters

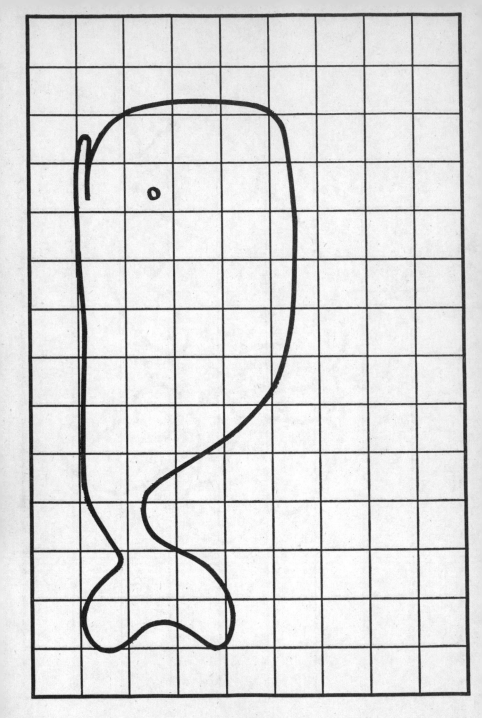

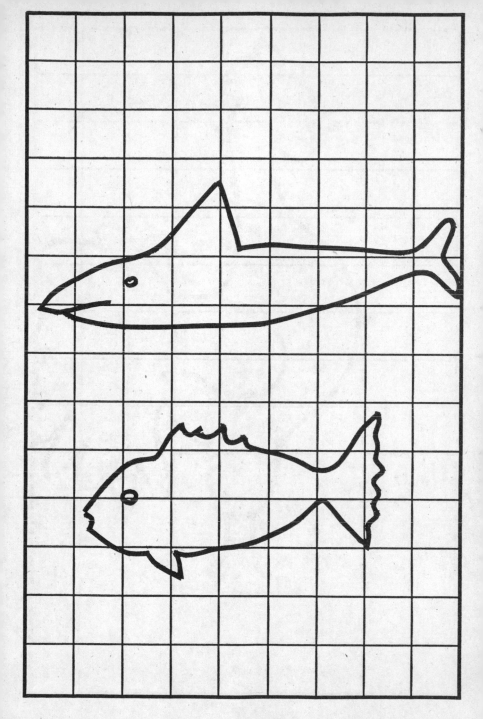

Christmas

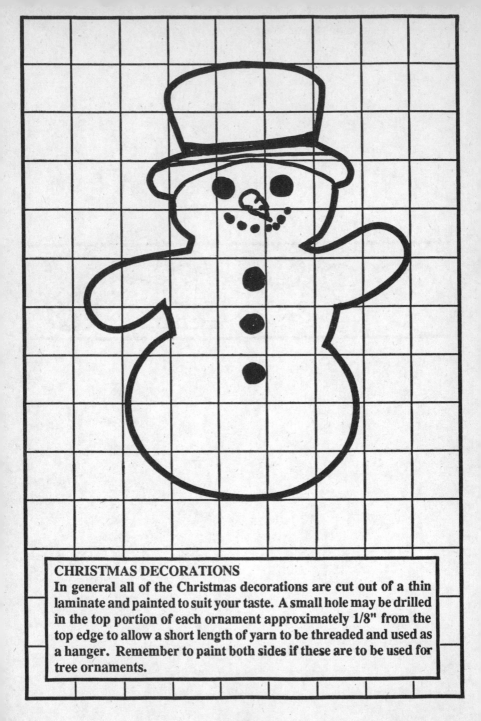

CHRISTMAS DECORATIONS
In general all of the Christmas decorations are cut out of a thin
laminate and painted to suit your taste. A small hole may be drilled
in the top portion of each ornament approximately 1/8" from the
top edge to allow a short length of yarn to be threaded and used as
a hanger. Remember to paint both sides if these are to be used for
tree ornaments.

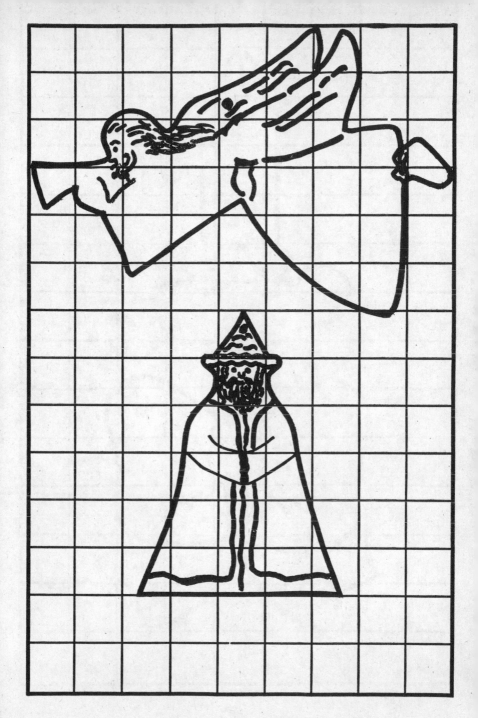

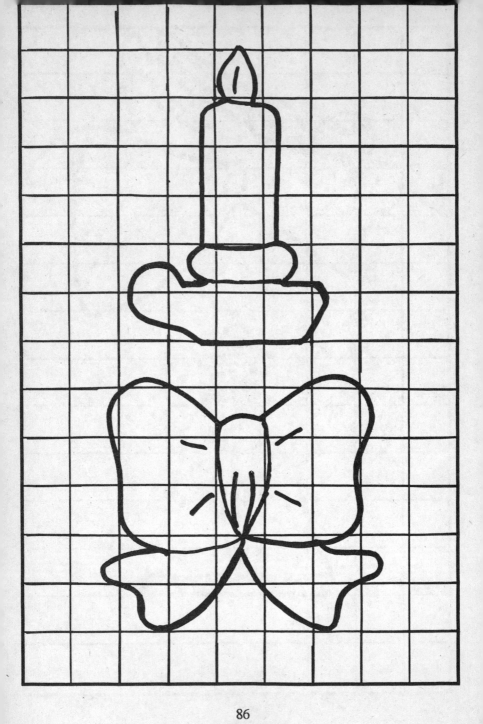

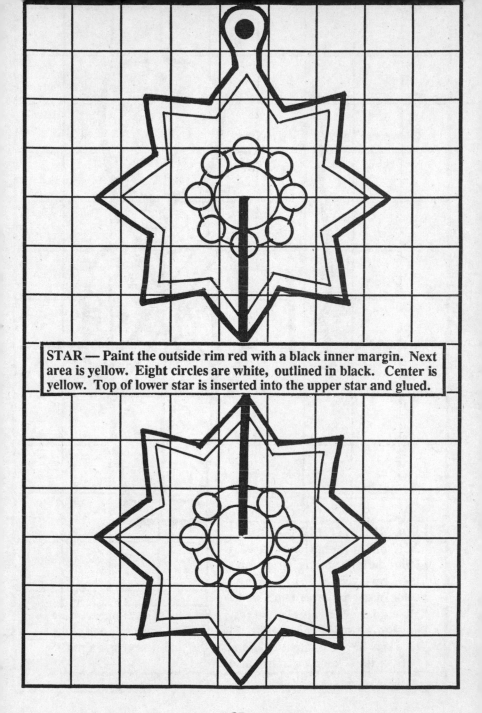

STAR — Paint the outside rim red with a black inner margin. Next area is yellow. Eight circles are white, outlined in black. Center is yellow. Top of lower star is inserted into the upper star and glued.

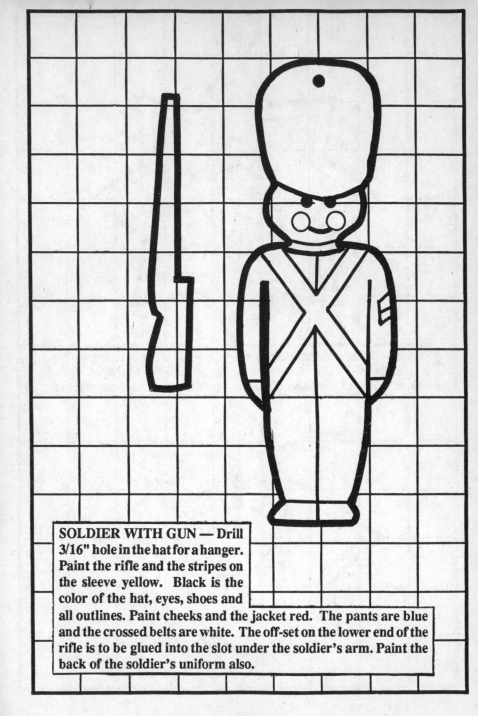

SOLDIER WITH GUN — Drill 3/16" hole in the hat for a hanger. Paint the rifle and the stripes on the sleeve yellow. Black is the color of the hat, eyes, shoes and all outlines. Paint cheeks and the jacket red. The pants are blue and the crossed belts are white. The off-set on the lower end of the rifle is to be glued into the slot under the soldier's arm. Paint the back of the soldier's uniform also.

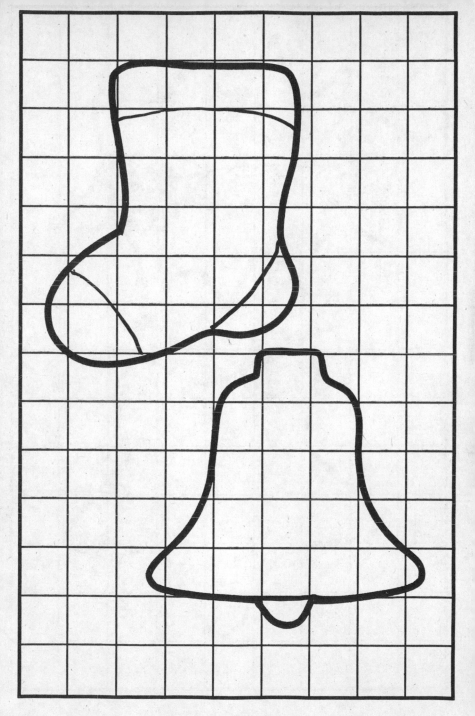

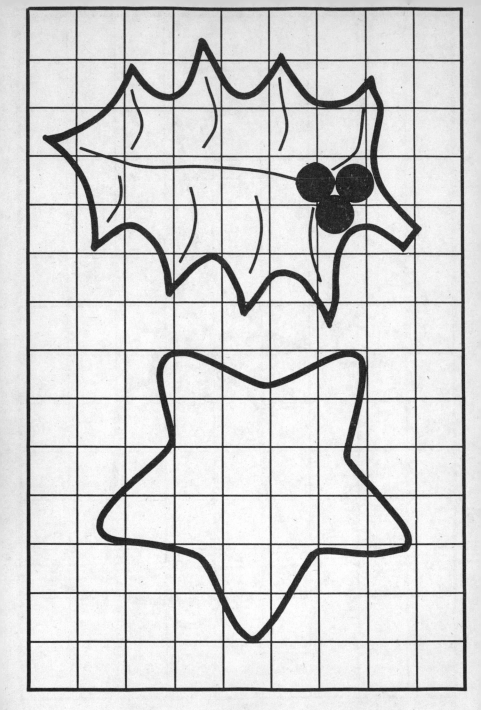

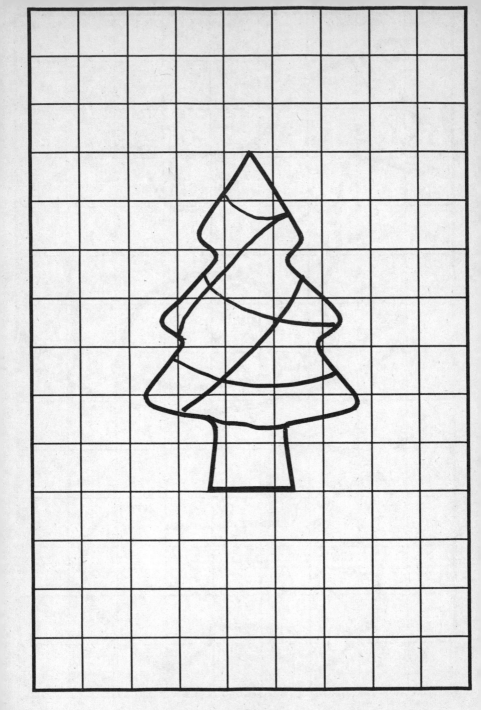

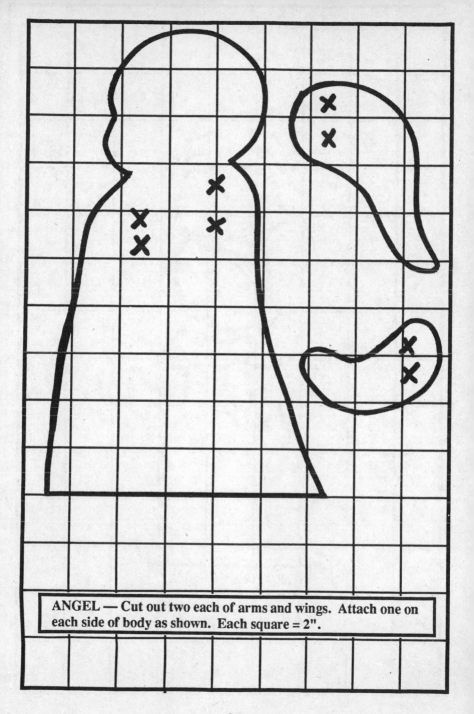

ANGEL — Cut out two each of arms and wings. Attach one on each side of body as shown. Each square = 2".

ELF – Each square = 2 ".

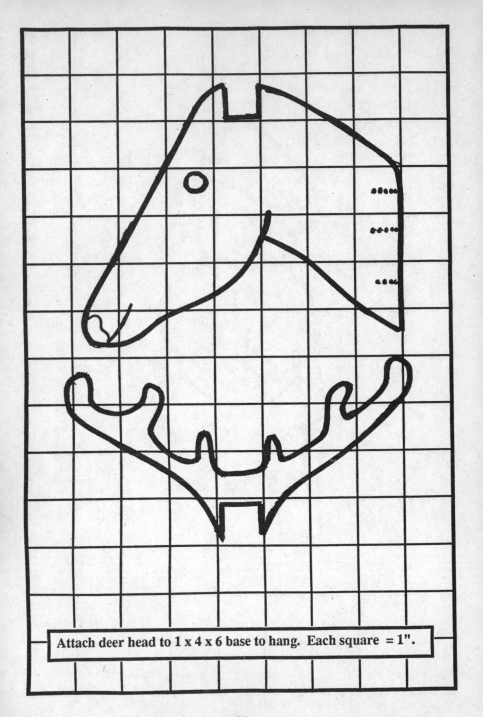

Attach deer head to 1 x 4 x 6 base to hang. Each square = 1".

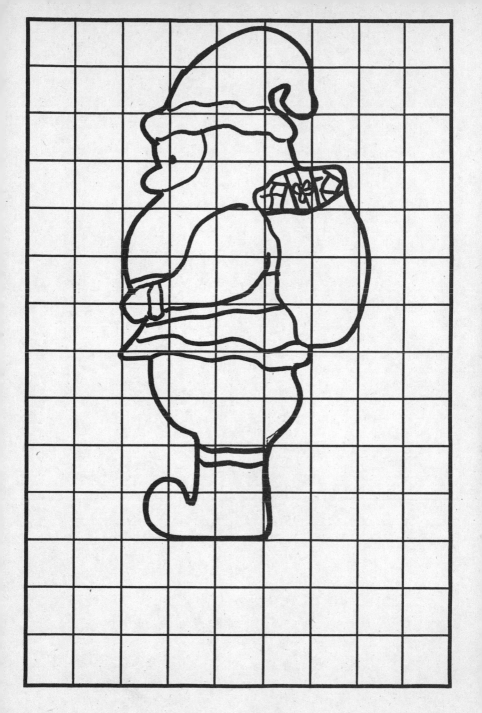

Fun to Make

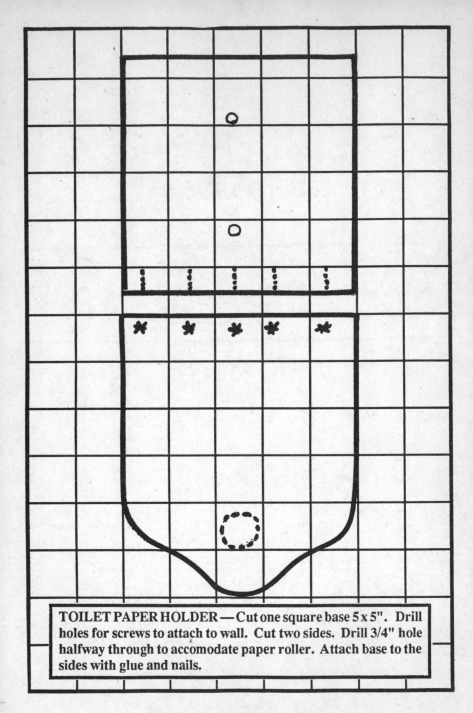

TOILET PAPER HOLDER — Cut one square base 5 x 5". Drill holes for screws to attach to wall. Cut two sides. Drill 3/4" hole halfway through to accomodate paper roller. Attach base to the sides with glue and nails.

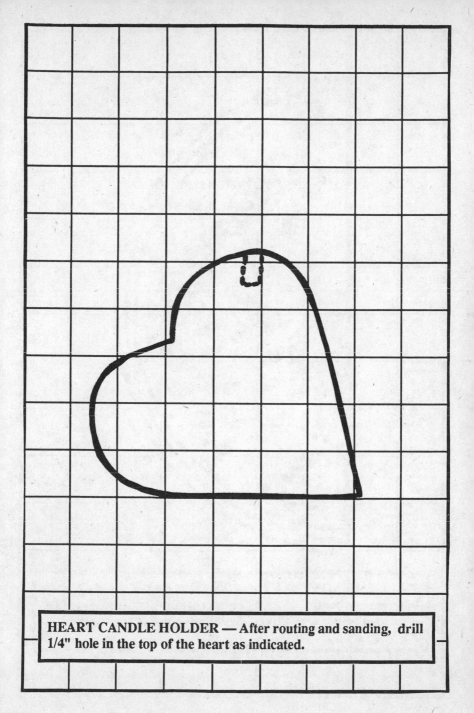

HEART CANDLE HOLDER — After routing and sanding, drill 1/4" hole in the top of the heart as indicated.

103

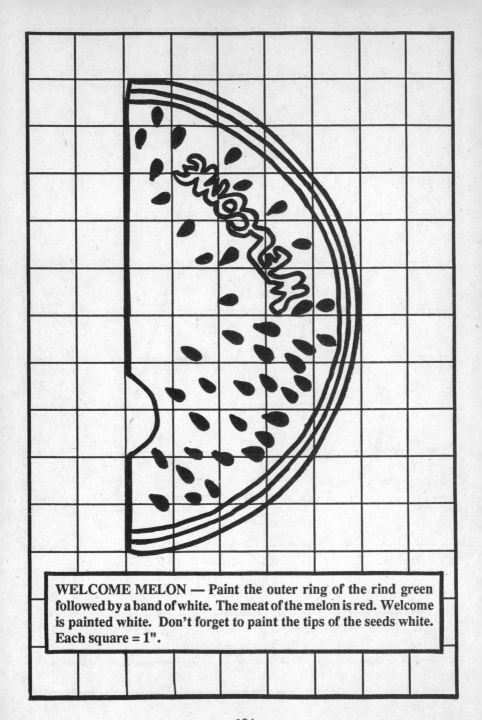

WELCOME MELON — Paint the outer ring of the rind green followed by a band of white. The meat of the melon is red. Welcome is painted white. Don't forget to paint the tips of the seeds white. Each square = 1".

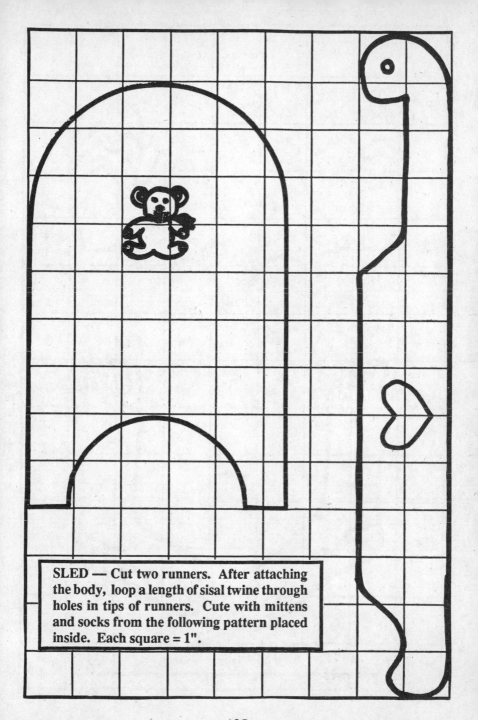

SLED — Cut two runners. After attaching the body, loop a length of sisal twine through holes in tips of runners. Cute with mittens and socks from the following pattern placed inside. Each square = 1".

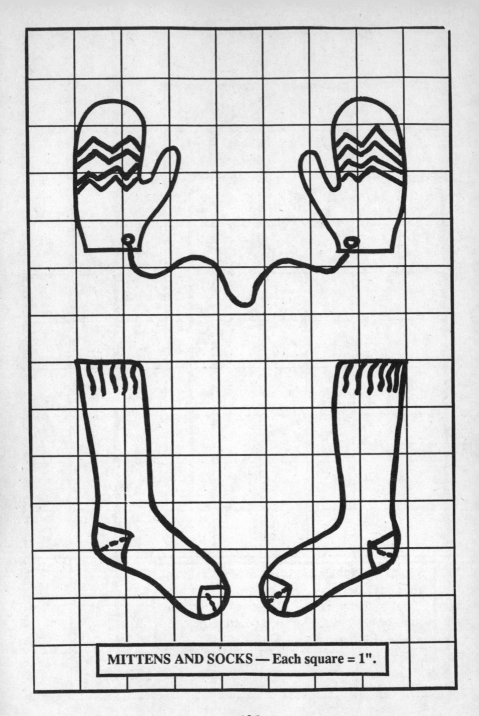

MITTENS AND SOCKS — Each square = 1".

From the Woods

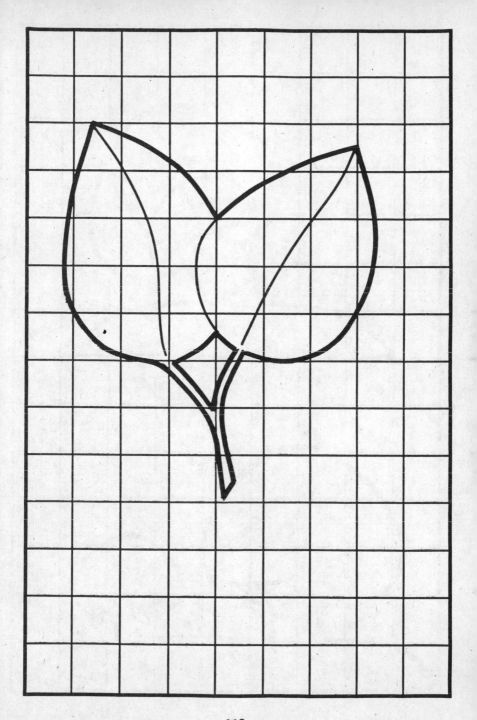

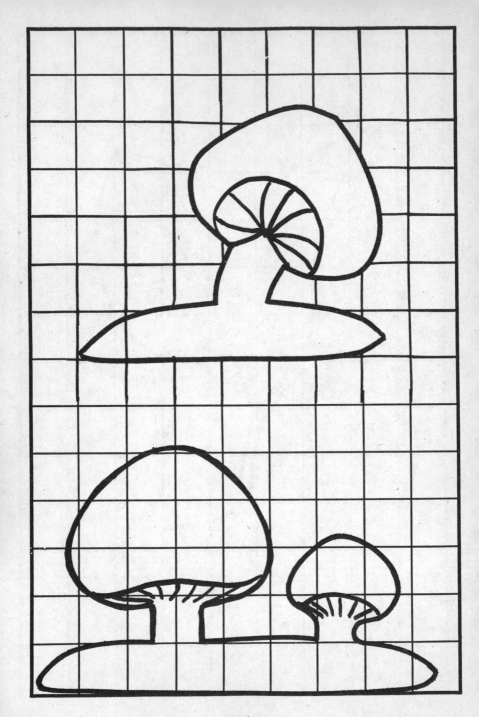

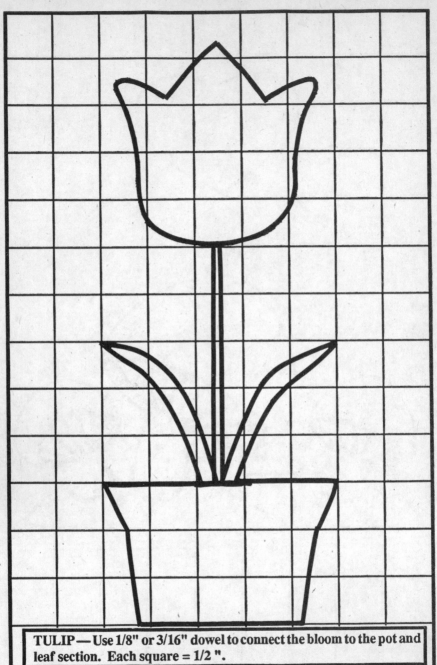

TULIP — Use 1/8" or 3/16" dowel to connect the bloom to the pot and leaf section. Each square = 1/2 ".

Music and Miscellaneous

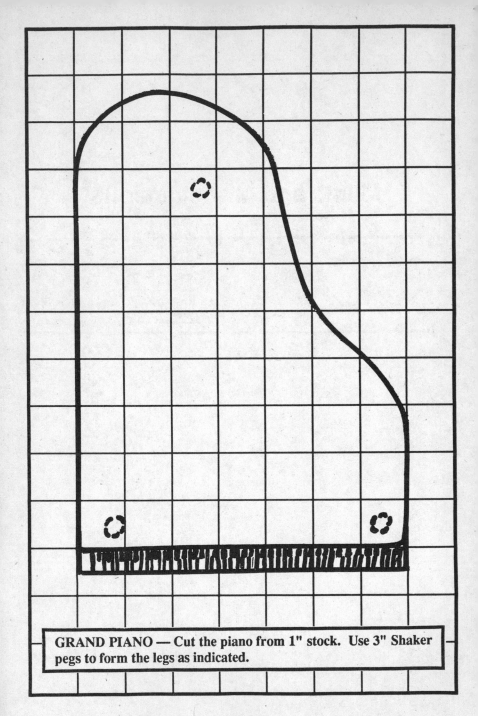

GRAND PIANO — Cut the piano from 1" stock. Use 3" Shaker pegs to form the legs as indicated.

118

STRINGED INSTRUMENTS — Strings for the Guitar, Banjo and Violin can either be painted, using a small brush, or you may choose to use black sewing thread, gluing at each end.

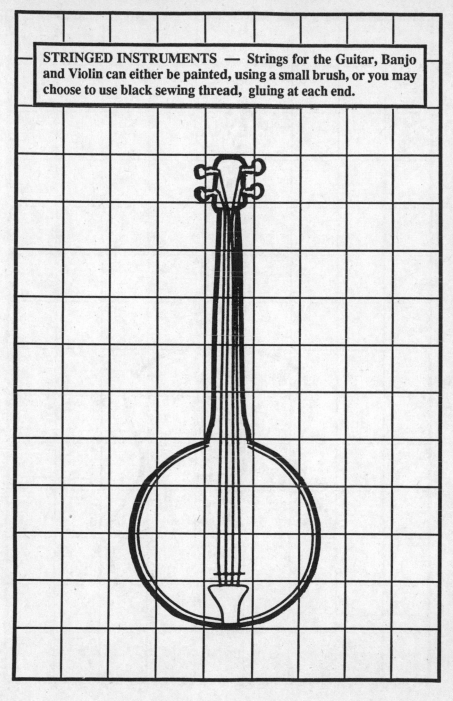

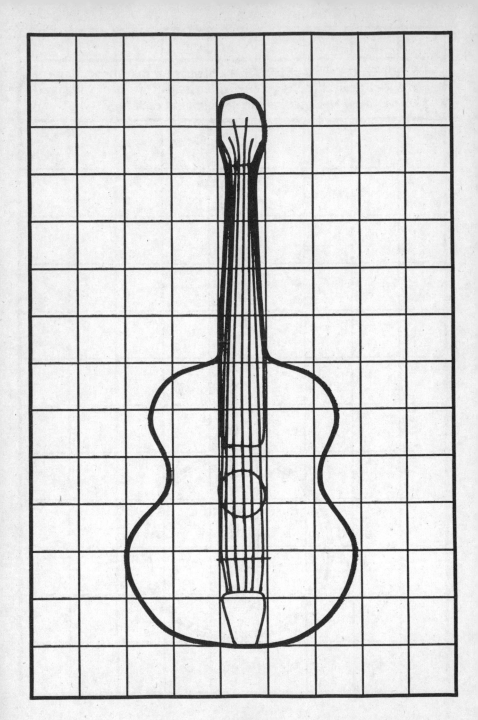

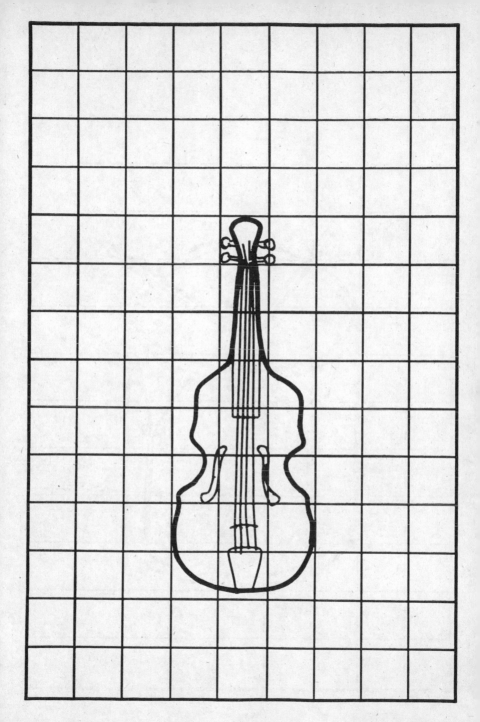

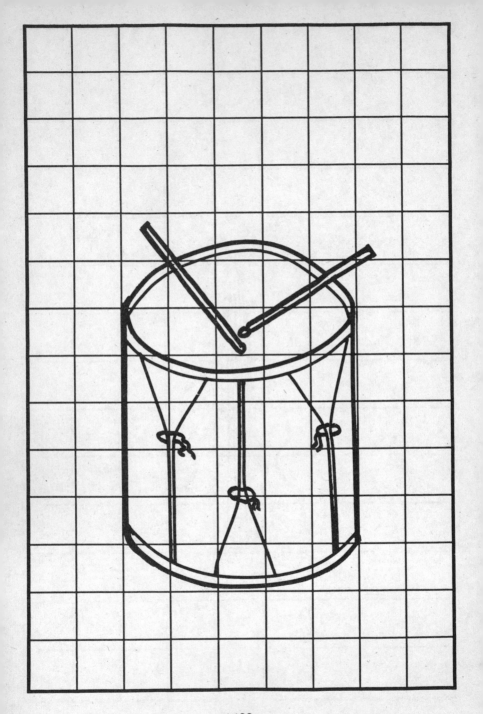

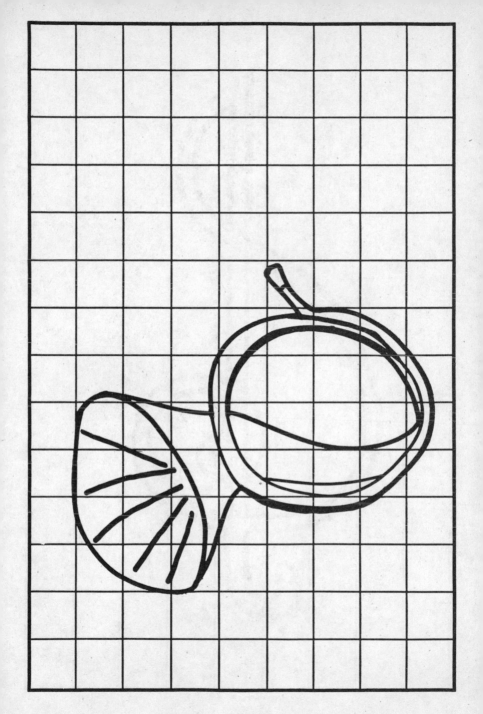

123

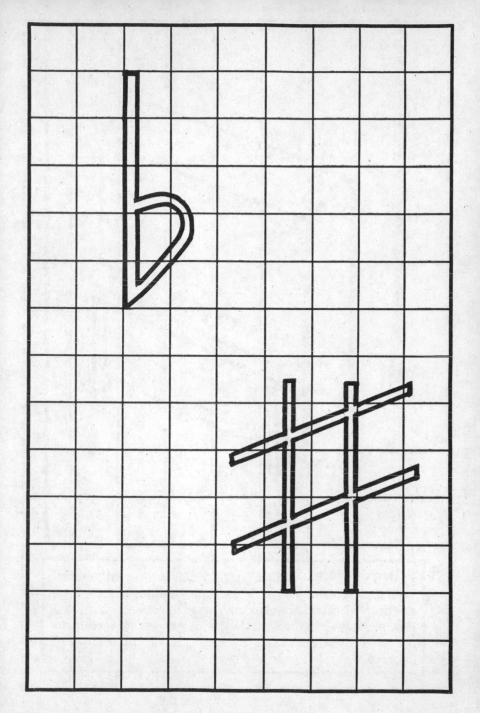

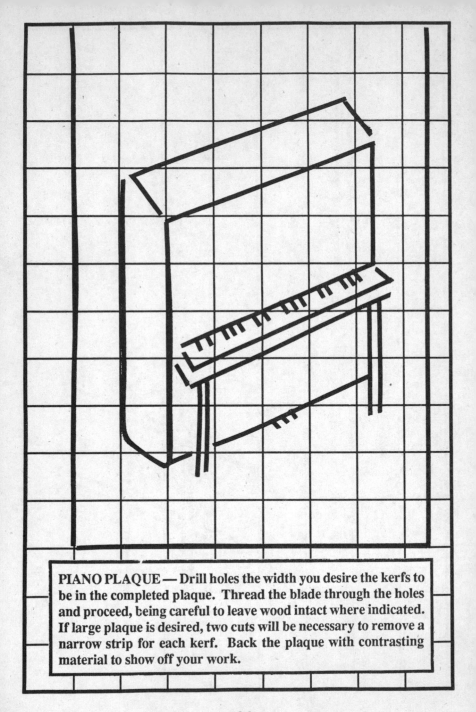

PIANO PLAQUE — Drill holes the width you desire the kerfs to be in the completed plaque. Thread the blade through the holes and proceed, being careful to leave wood intact where indicated. If large plaque is desired, two cuts will be necessary to remove a narrow strip for each kerf. Back the plaque with contrasting material to show off your work.

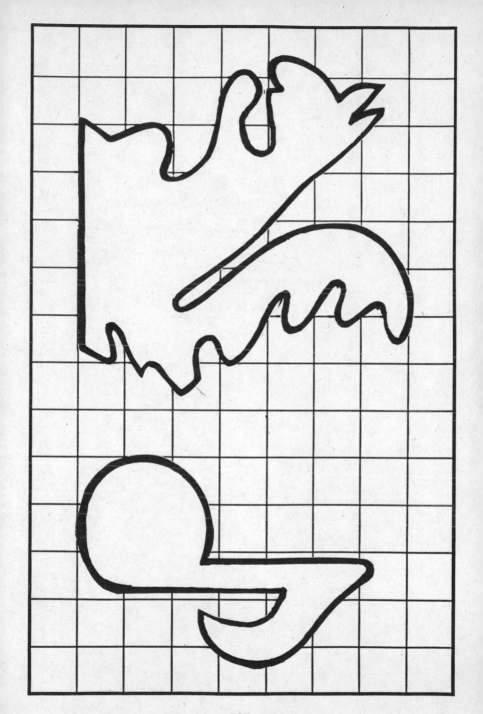

Street Scenes

STREET SCENE—All buildings and other items should be made from the same size stock (2"x 4", 1"x 4", etc.) Gable roofs as indicated.

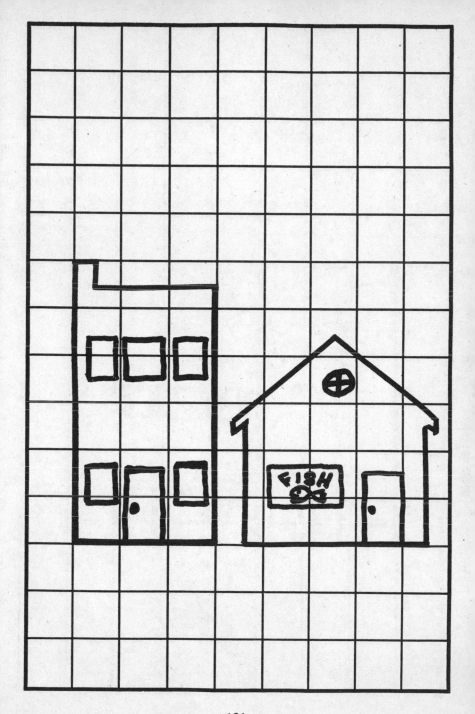

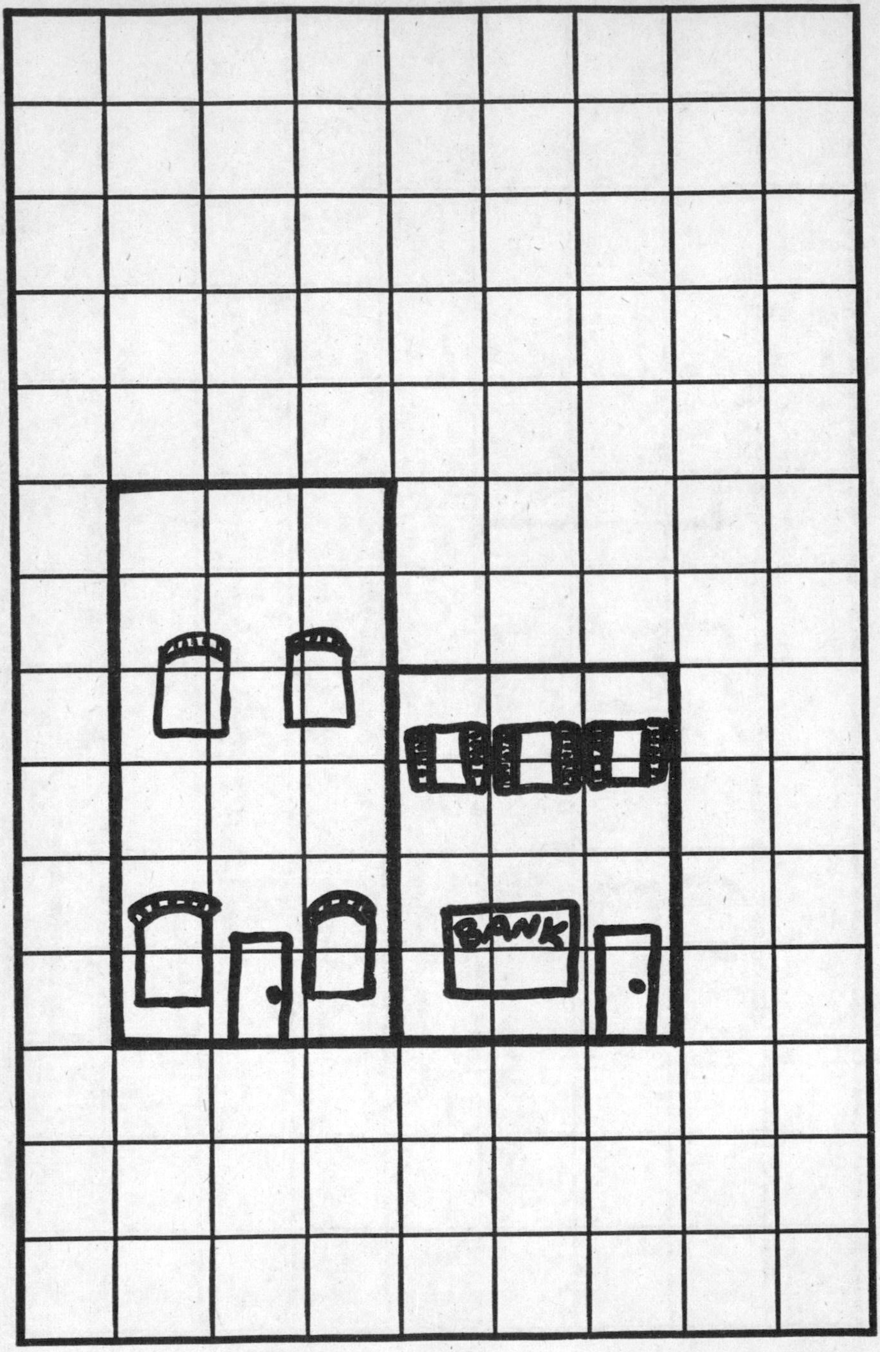
BANK

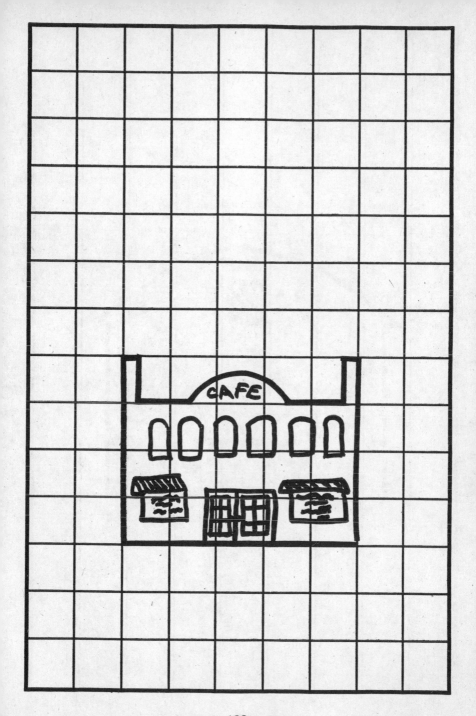

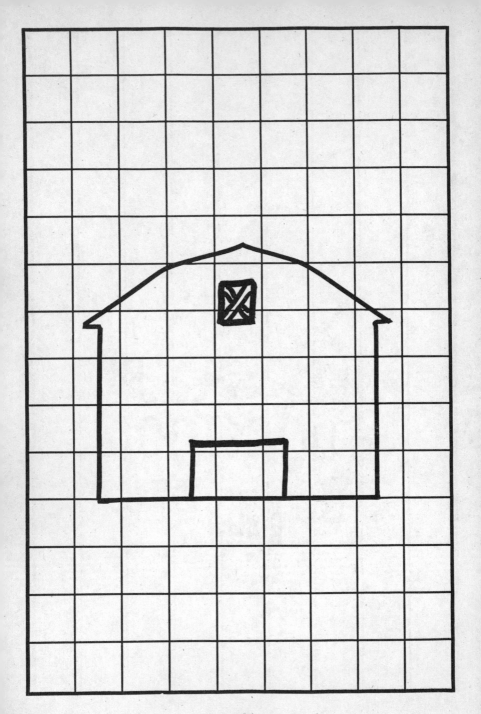

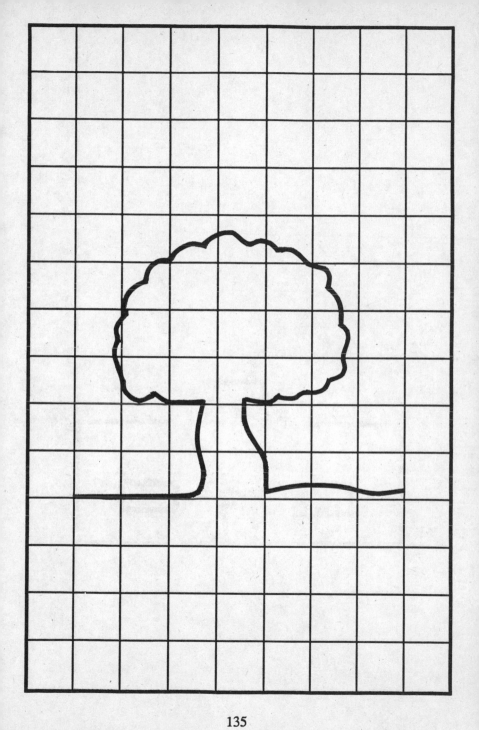

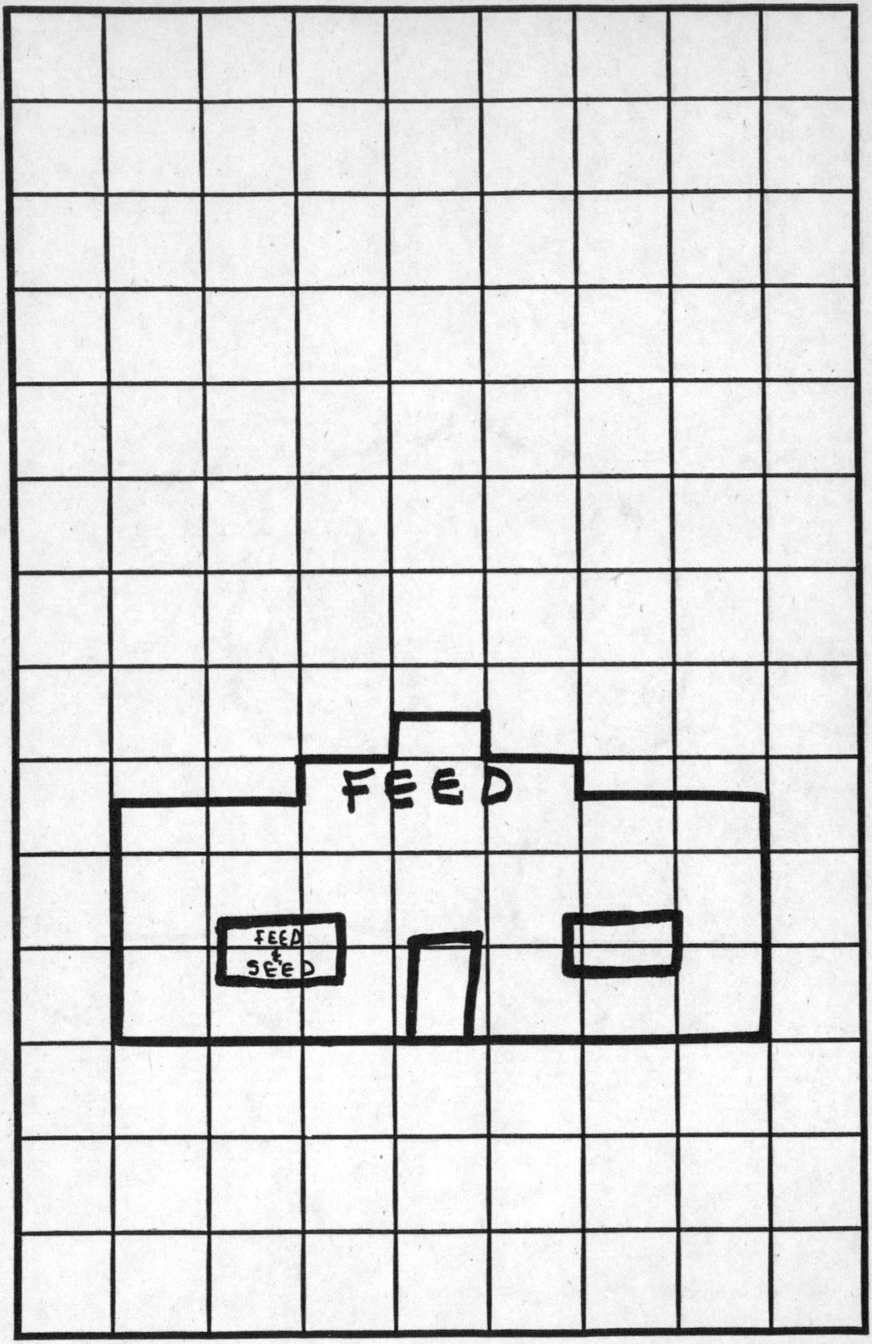
FEED
FEED
&
SEED

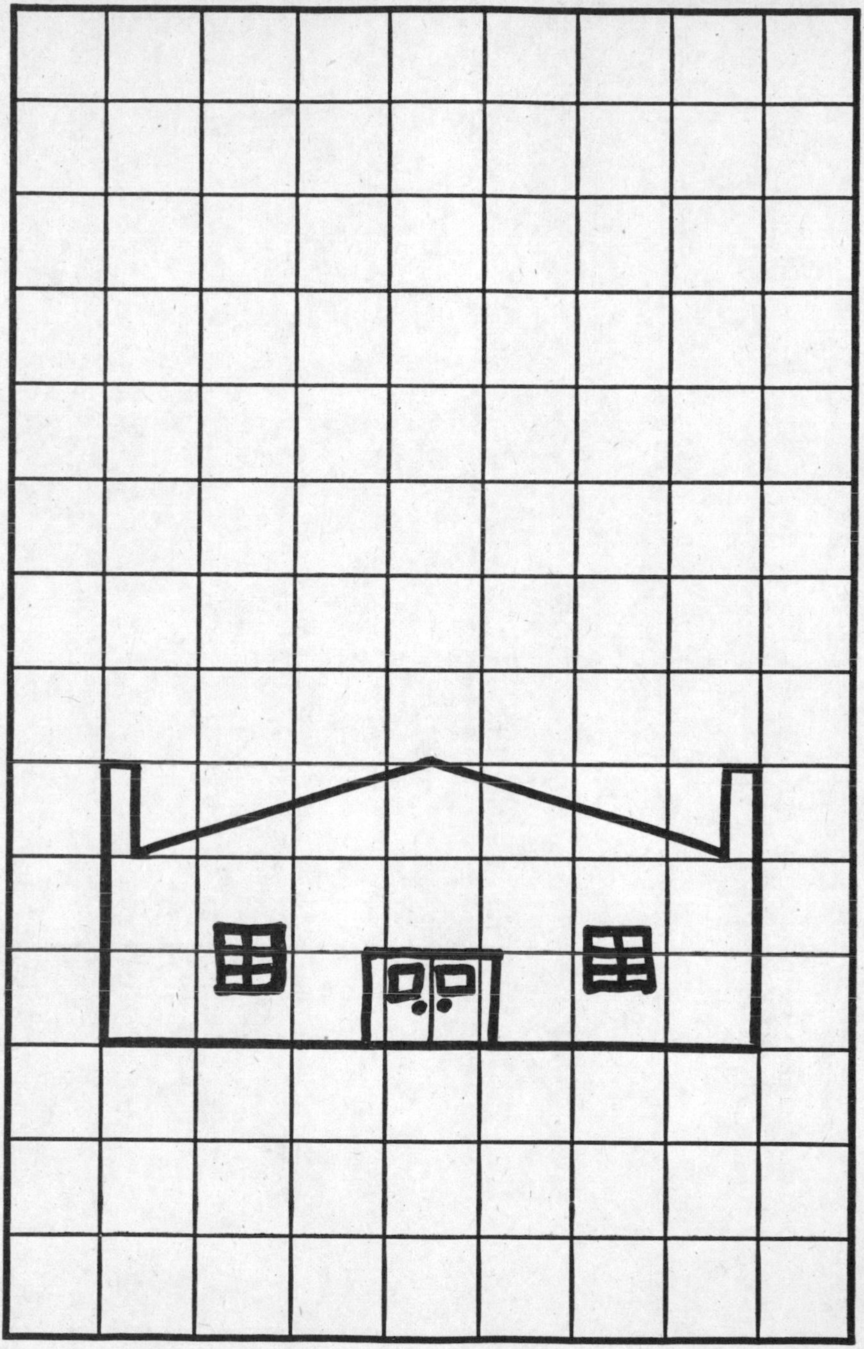

Handy Household Helpers

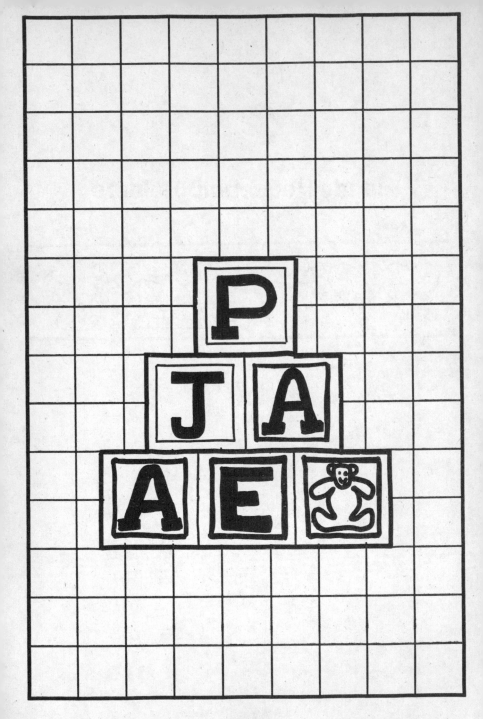

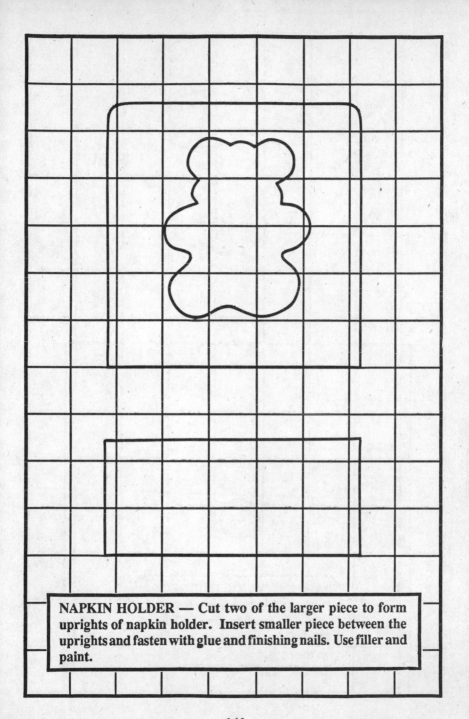

NAPKIN HOLDER — Cut two of the larger piece to form uprights of napkin holder. Insert smaller piece between the uprights and fasten with glue and finishing nails. Use filler and paint.

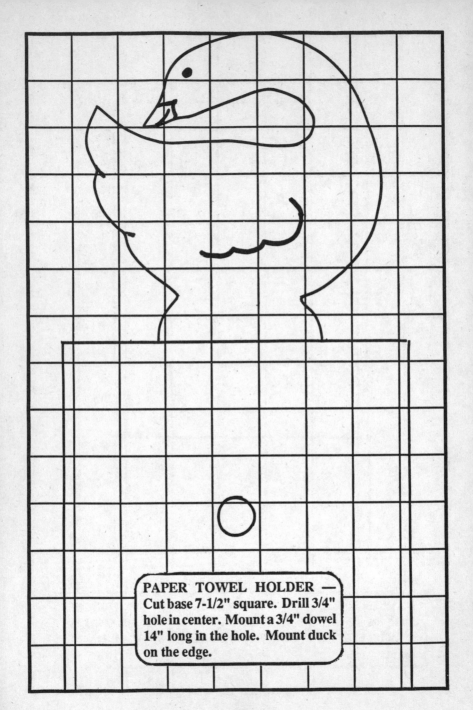

PAPER TOWEL HOLDER —
Cut base 7-1/2" square. Drill 3/4" hole in center. Mount a 3/4" dowel 14" long in the hole. Mount duck on the edge.

Cross Cuts

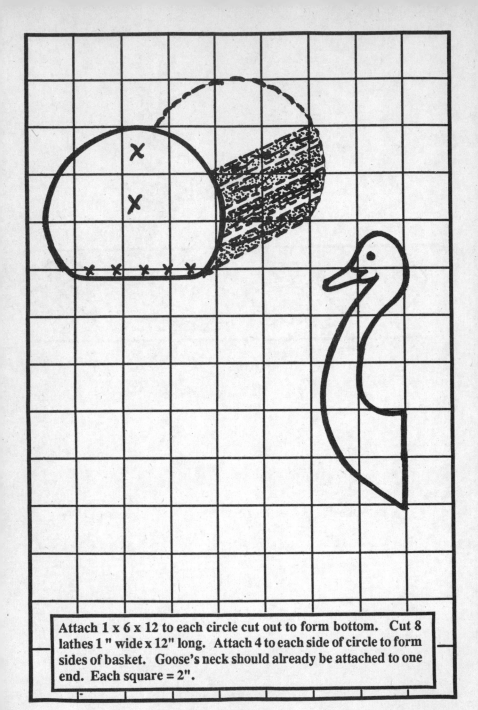

Attach 1 x 6 x 12 to each circle cut out to form bottom. Cut 8 lathes 1 " wide x 12" long. Attach 4 to each side of circle to form sides of basket. Goose's neck should already be attached to one end. Each square = 2".

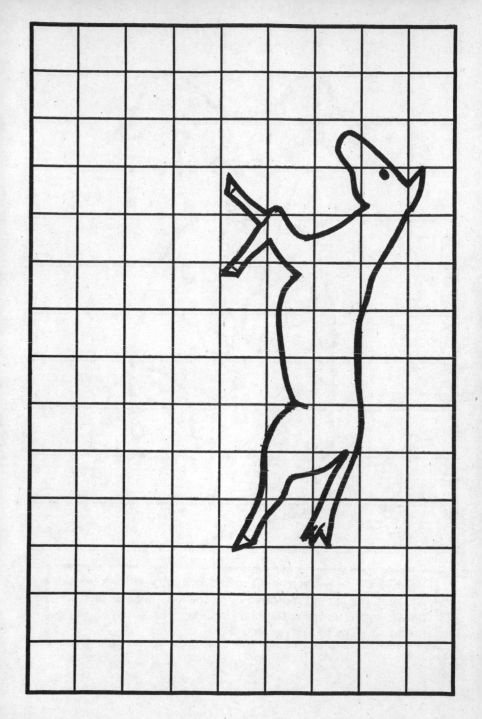

DOOR STOP — Attach wedge to back of bunny with white glue and finishing nails as indicated by *. (Follow the same instructions using the wedge for the following 3 pages for bunny, dog and bear door stops.) Each square = 2 in.

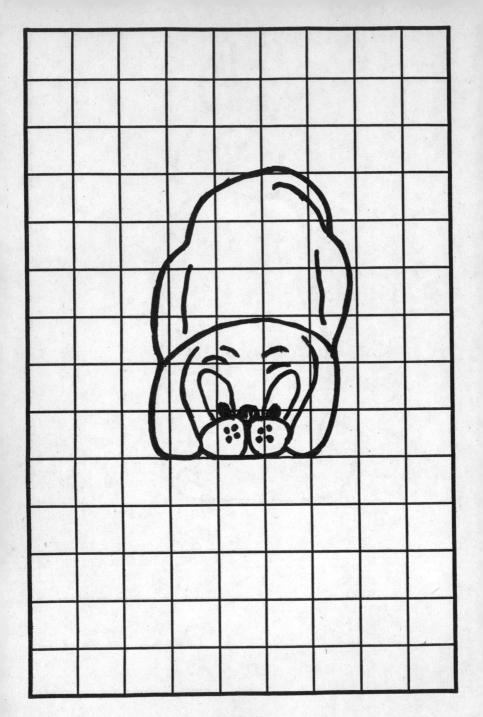

SHELF SITTERS — Let these cats peek over the edge of your shelves.

Attach cat's head to body with glue and finishing nails.

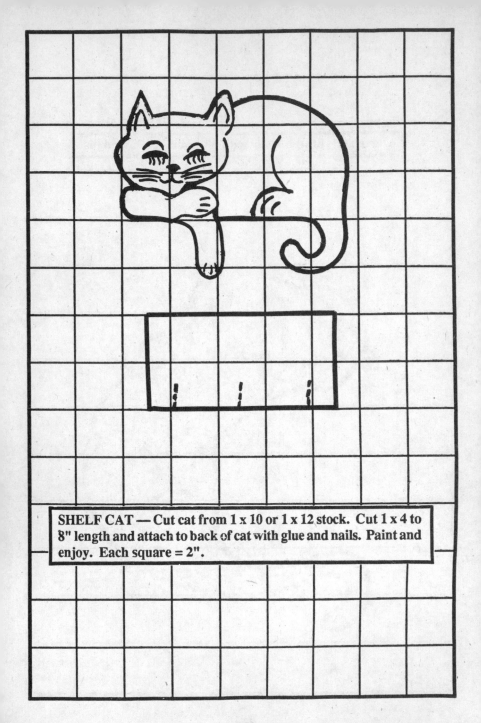

SHELF CAT — Cut cat from 1 x 10 or 1 x 12 stock. Cut 1 x 4 to 8" length and attach to back of cat with glue and nails. Paint and enjoy. Each square = 2".

Cut out one body and 2 each arms and legs. Attach with white glue and finishing nails.

BUNNY PULL TOY — Attach bunny to base as shown. Attach wheels with 1/4" wheel hubs as shown. Cord attached to front of base completes the pull toy. Each square = 2".

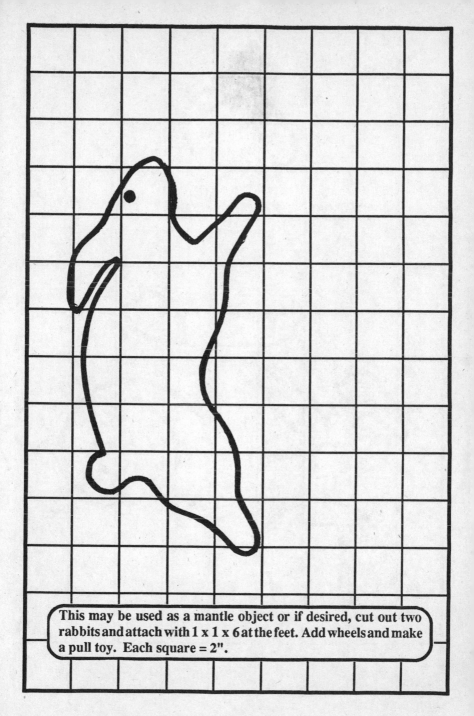

This may be used as a mantle object or if desired, cut out two rabbits and attach with 1 x 1 x 6 at the feet. Add wheels and make a pull toy. Each square = 2".

Toys and Games

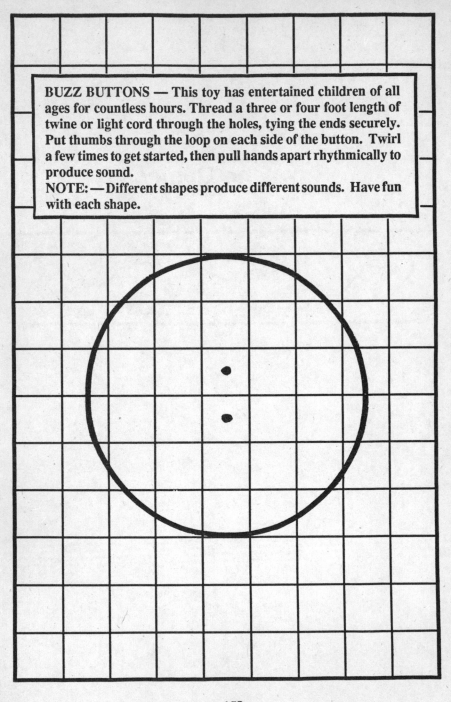

BUZZ BUTTONS — This toy has entertained children of all ages for countless hours. Thread a three or four foot length of twine or light cord through the holes, tying the ends securely. Put thumbs through the loop on each side of the button. Twirl a few times to get started, then pull hands apart rhythmically to produce sound.

NOTE: — Different shapes produce different sounds. Have fun with each shape.

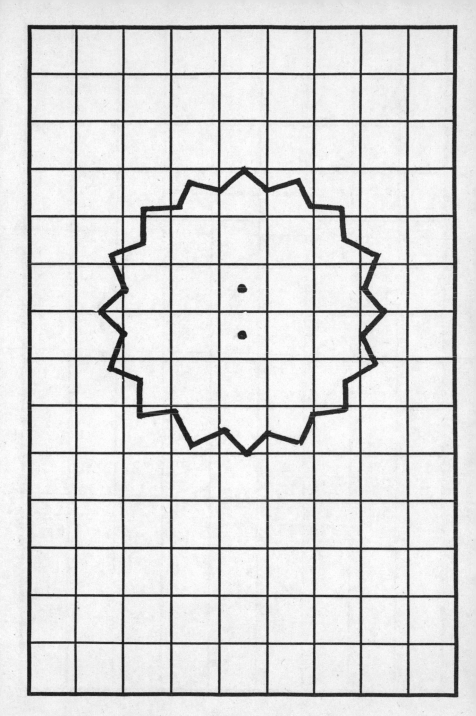

159

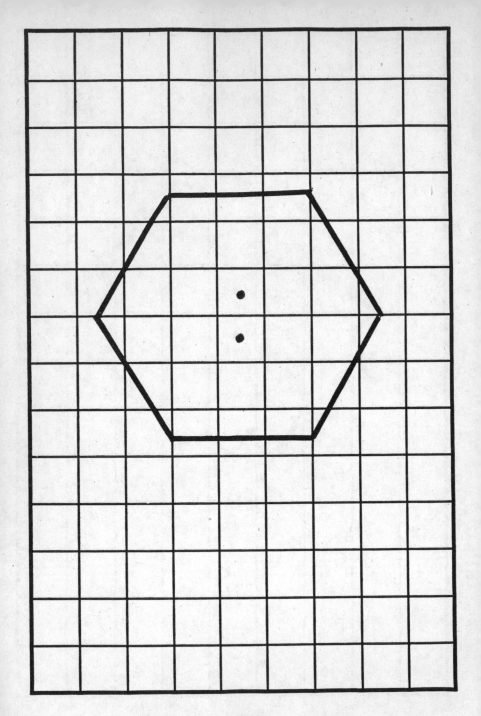

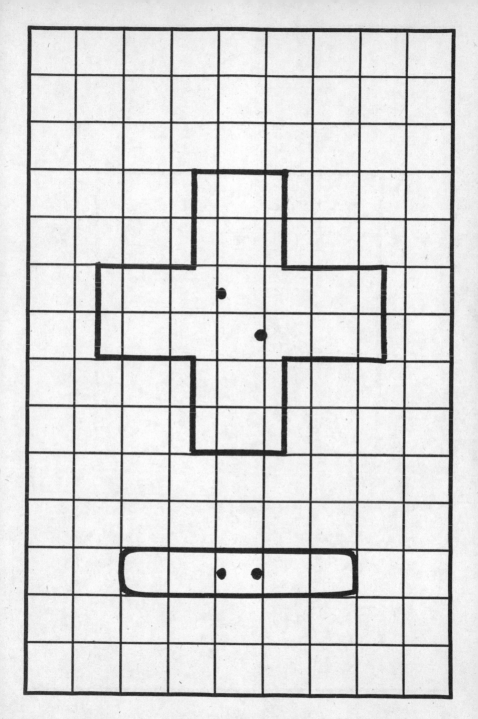

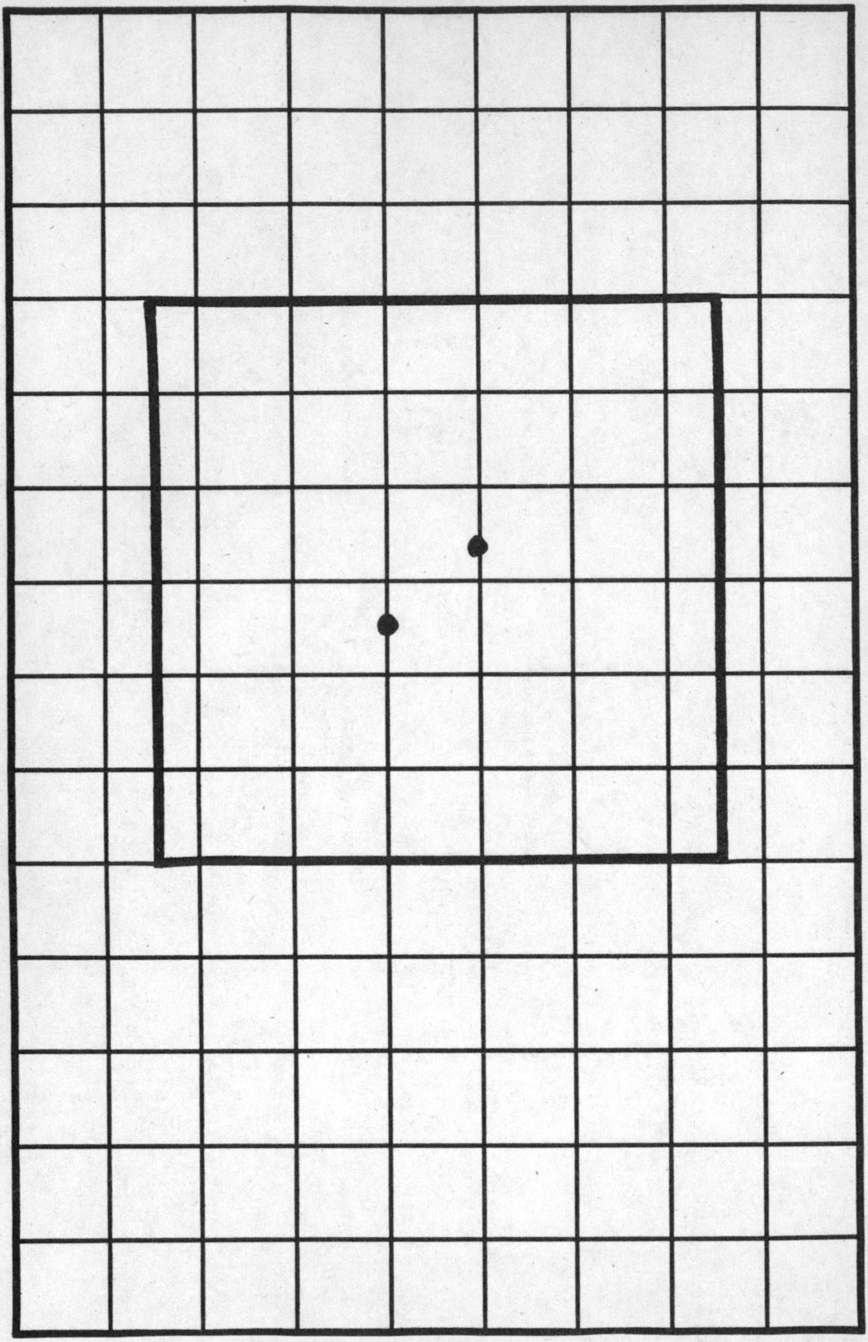

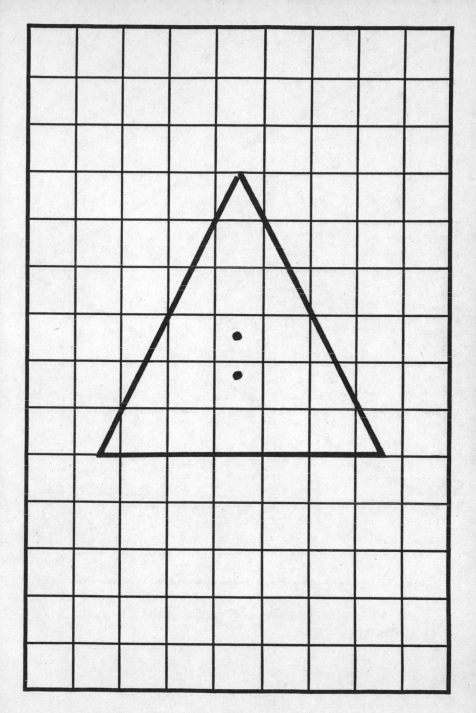

GAME—Drill 3/16" holes 1/2" deep as indicated. Place 14 golf tees in the holes. Object is to "jump" tees and remove them, leaving only one tee.

164

TIC TAC TOE — Drill 1/4" deep holes as indicated. Use 5 light and 5 dark colored marbles as playing pieces.

YO-YO — Cut two rounds from 1"x 4" stock. Drill 3/16" diameter hole 1/4" deep in each round. Be sure to center each hole. Rout both sides of each round with 1/4" round-over bit. Cut 3/16" dowel to 3/4" length. Fit rounds together with dowel. Three to four foot length of string completes the toy.

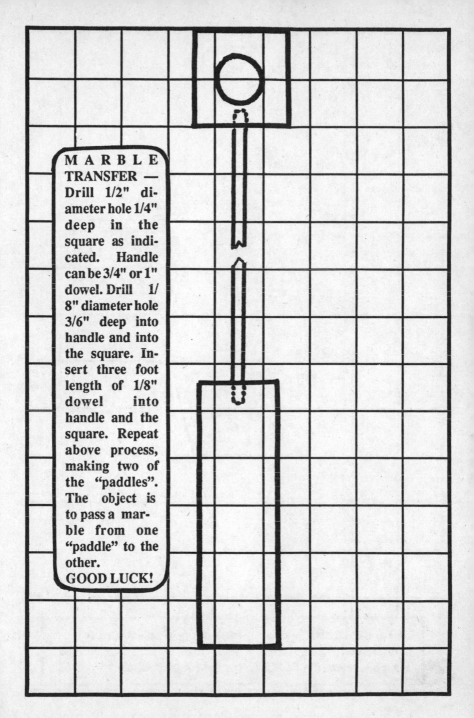

MARBLE TRANSFER — Drill 1/2" diameter hole 1/4" deep in the square as indicated. Handle can be 3/4" or 1" dowel. Drill 1/8" diameter hole 3/6" deep into handle and into the square. Insert three foot length of 1/8" dowel into handle and the square. Repeat above process, making two of the "paddles". The object is to pass a marble from one "paddle" to the other. GOOD LUCK!

167

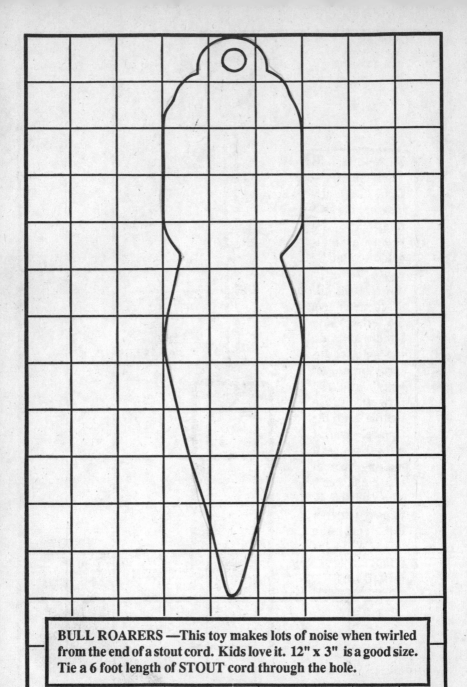

BULL ROARERS —This toy makes lots of noise when twirled from the end of a stout cord. Kids love it. 12" x 3" is a good size. Tie a 6 foot length of STOUT cord through the hole.

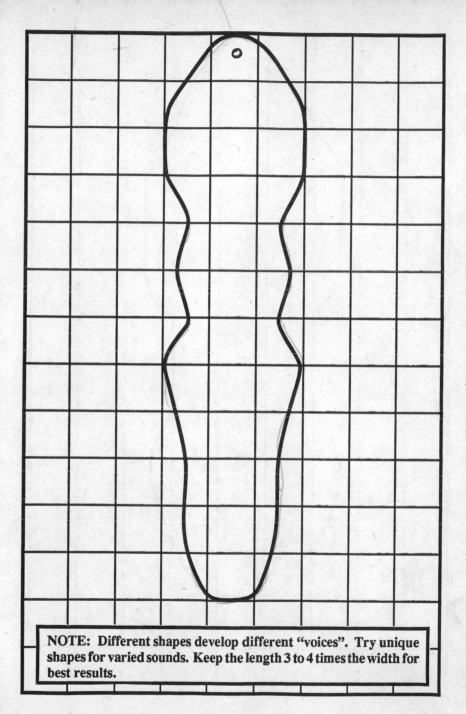

NOTE: Different shapes develop different "voices". Try unique shapes for varied sounds. Keep the length 3 to 4 times the width for best results.

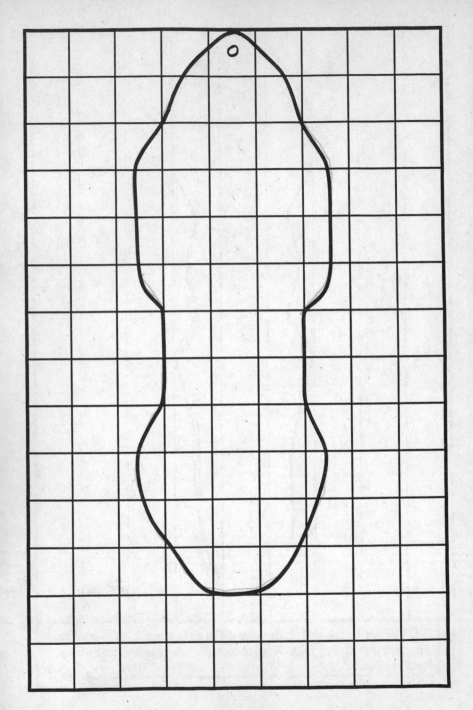

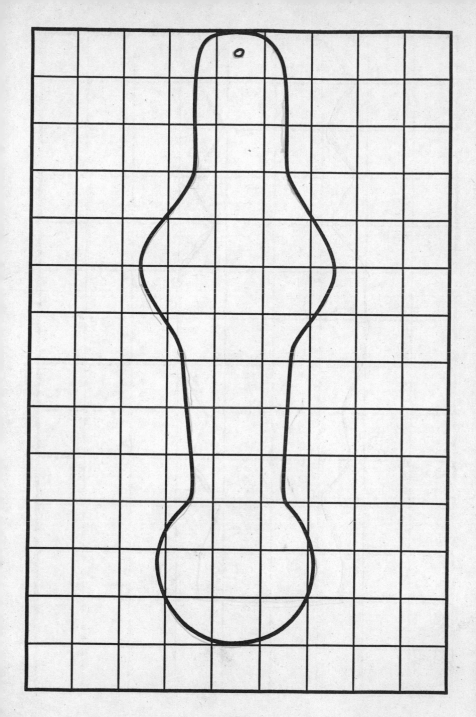

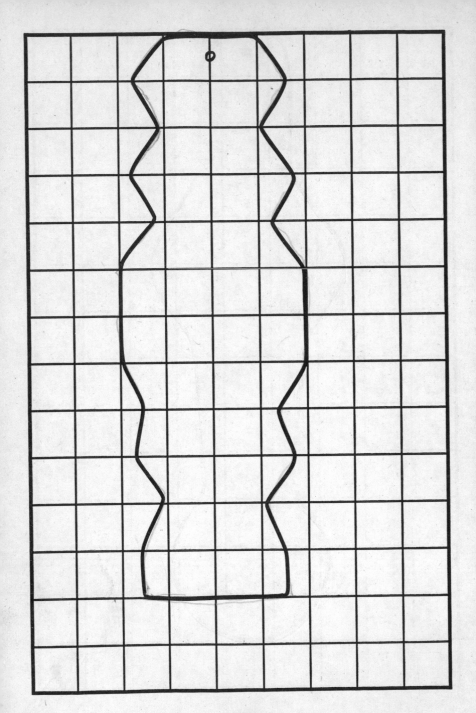

172

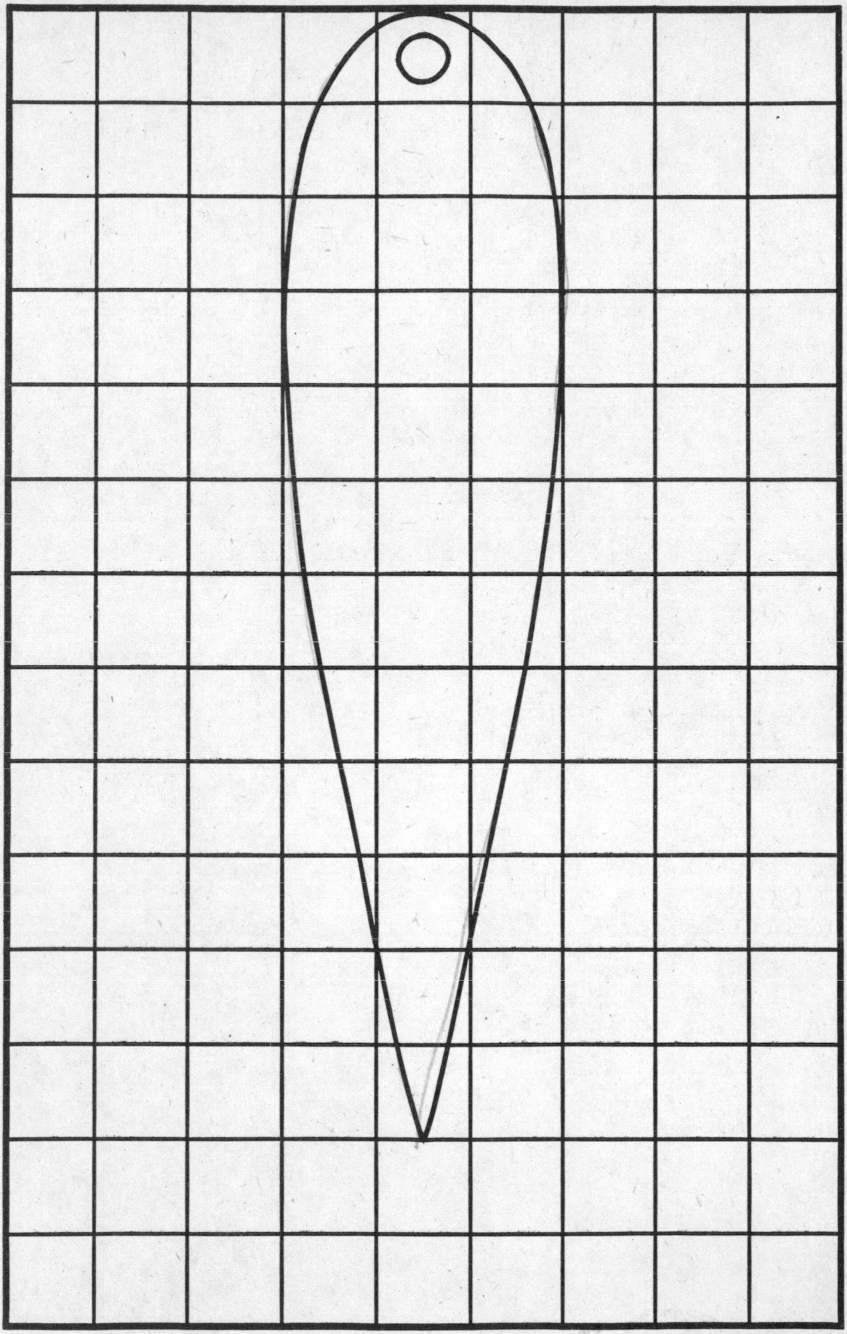

U.S.A.

175

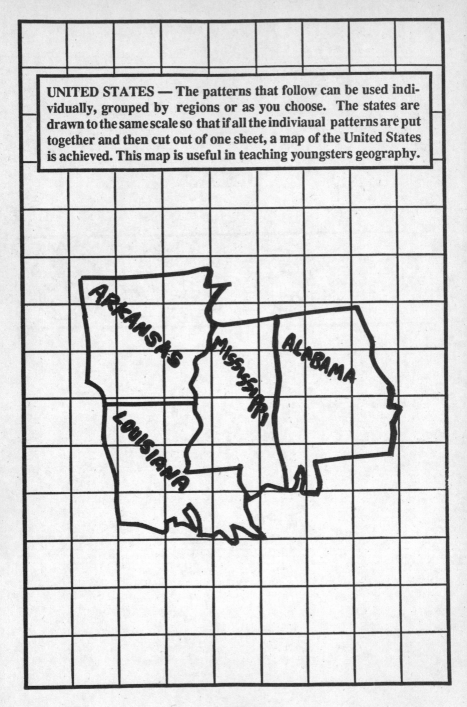

UNITED STATES — The patterns that follow can be used individually, grouped by regions or as you choose. The states are drawn to the same scale so that if all the indiviaual patterns are put together and then cut out of one sheet, a map of the United States is achieved. This map is useful in teaching youngsters geography.

ARKANSAS

MISSISSIPPI

ALABAMA

LOUISIANA

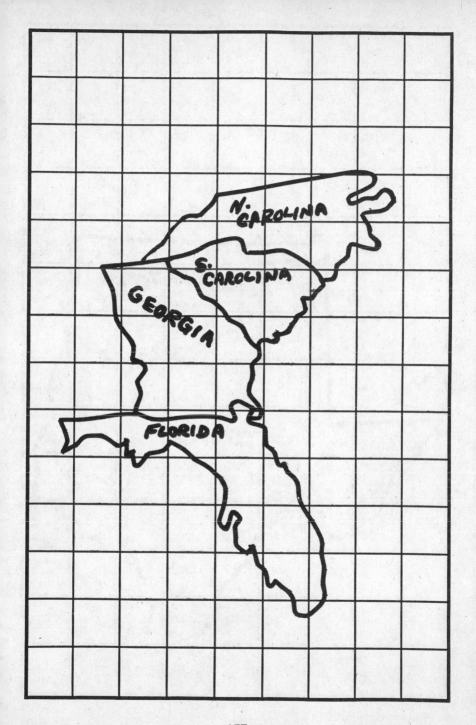

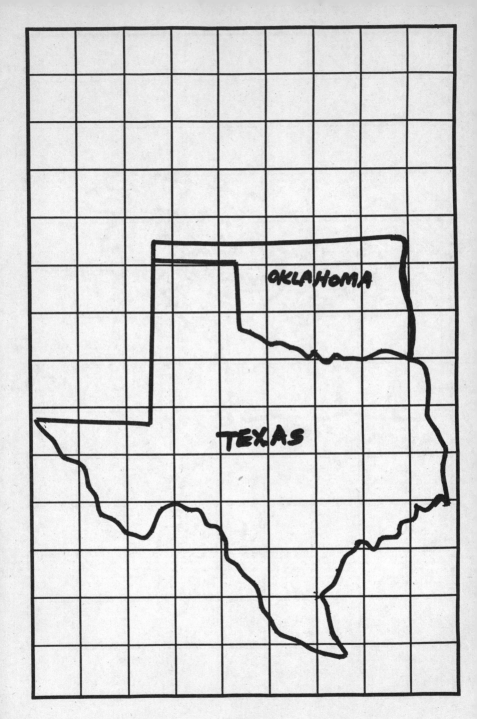

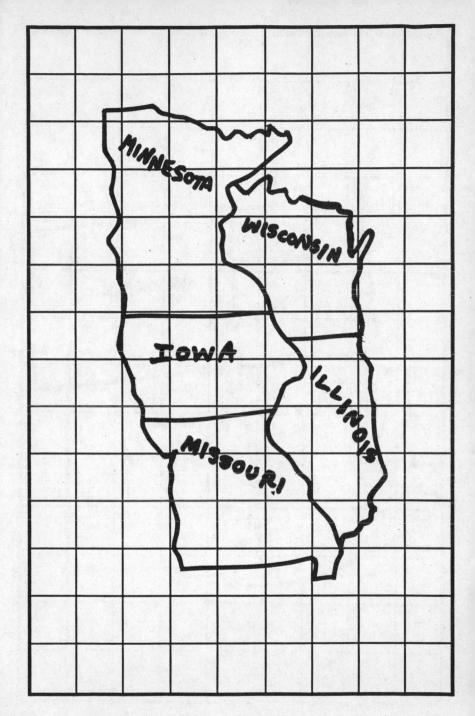

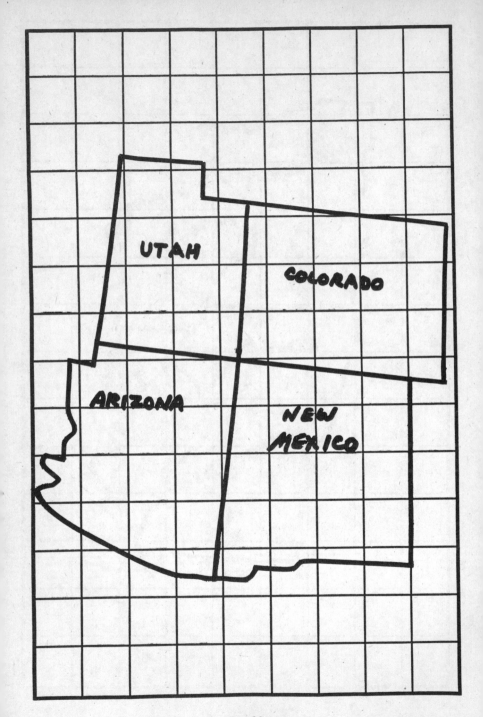

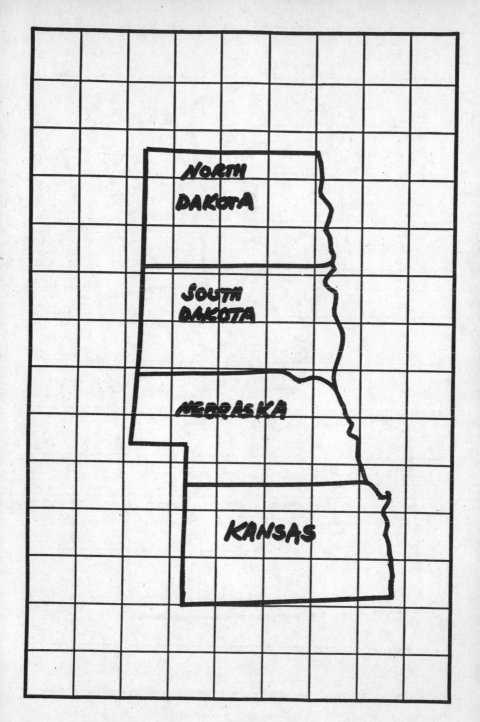

NORTH DAKOTA

SOUTH DAKOTA

NEBRASKA

KANSAS

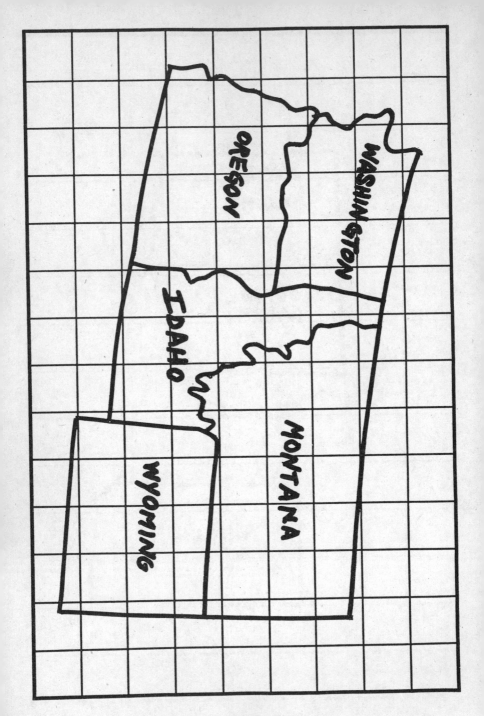

182

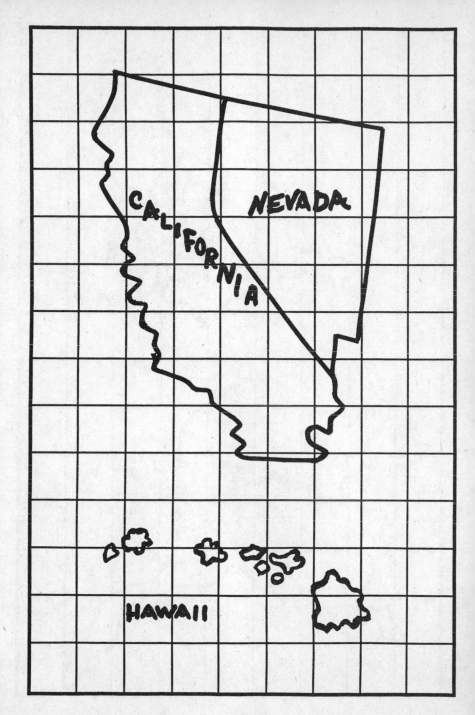

CALIFORNIA

NEVADA

HAWAII

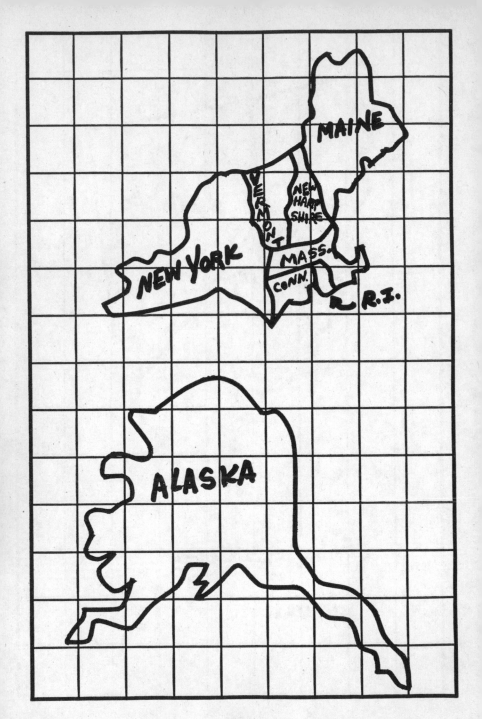

MAINE

VERMONT

NEW HAMPSHIRE

NEW YORK

MASS.

CONN.

R.I.

ALASKA

184

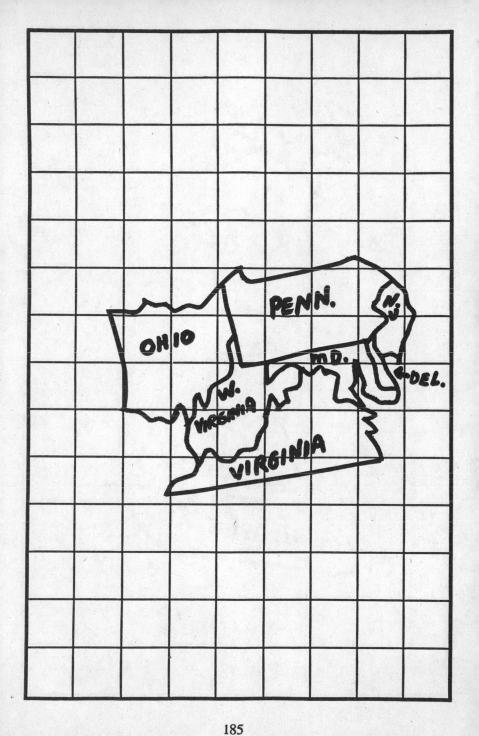

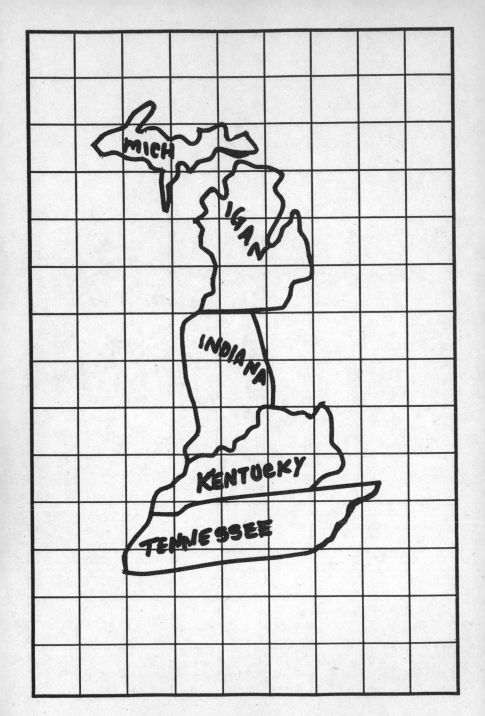

Shelves and Plaques

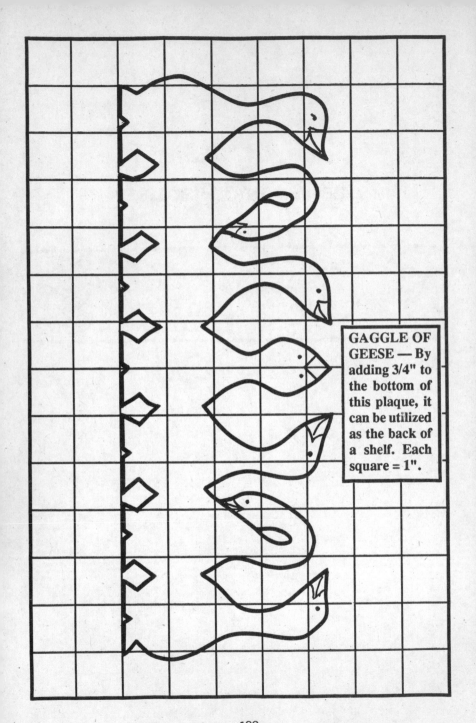

GAGGLE OF GEESE — By adding 3/4" to the bottom of this plaque, it can be utilized as the back of a shelf. Each square = 1".

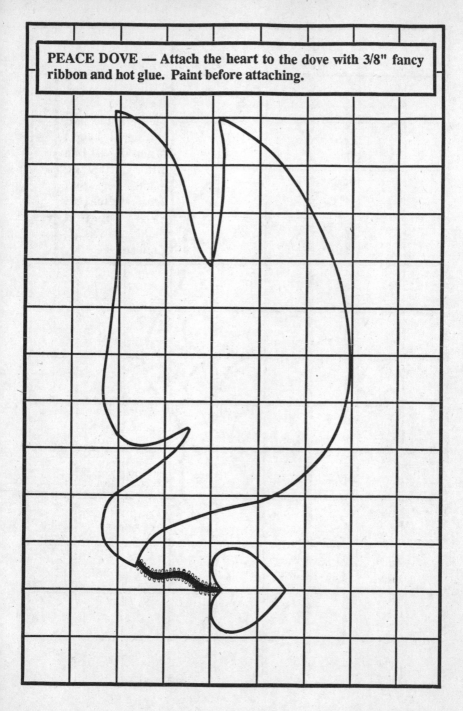

PEACE DOVE — Attach the heart to the dove with 3/8" fancy ribbon and hot glue. Paint before attaching.

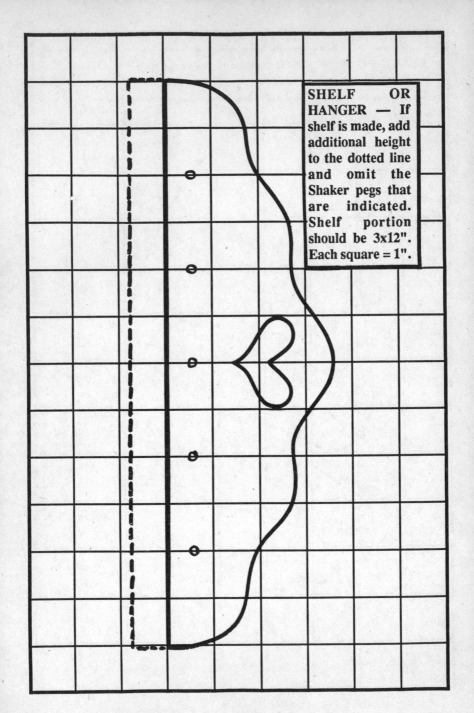

SHELF OR HANGER — If shelf is made, add additional height to the dotted line and omit the Shaker pegs that are indicated. Shelf portion should be 3x12". Each square = 1".

SHELF BRACKET — Each square = 1".

191

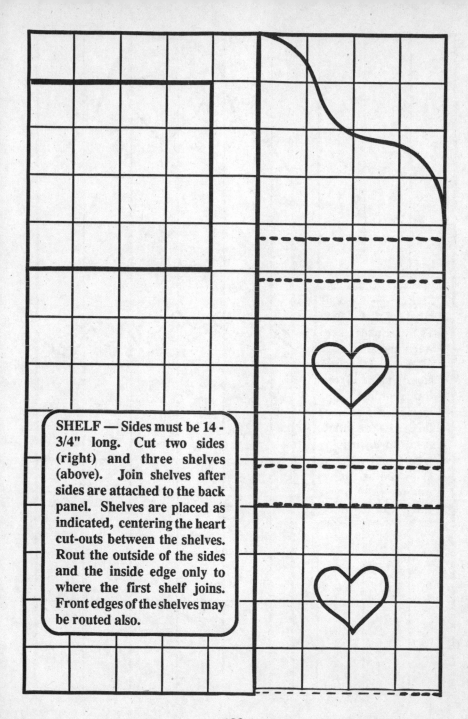

SHELF — Sides must be 14 - 3/4" long. Cut two sides (right) and three shelves (above). Join shelves after sides are attached to the back panel. Shelves are placed as indicated, centering the heart cut-outs between the shelves. Rout the outside of the sides and the inside edge only to where the first shelf joins. Front edges of the shelves may be routed also.

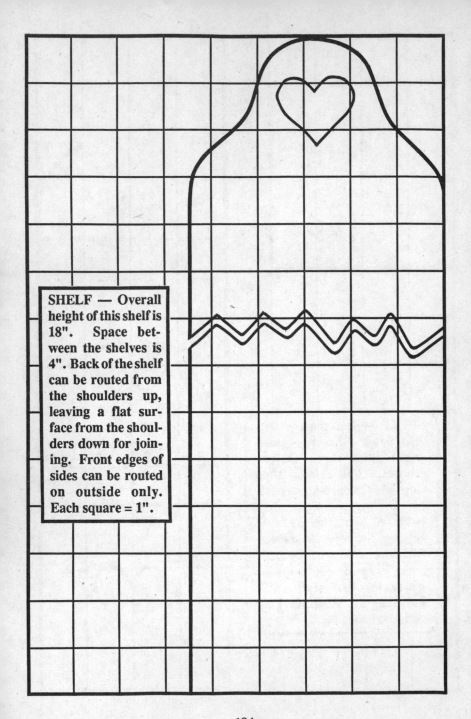

SHELF — Overall height of this shelf is 18". Space between the shelves is 4". Back of the shelf can be routed from the shoulders up, leaving a flat surface from the shoulders down for joining. Front edges of sides can be routed on outside only. Each square = 1".

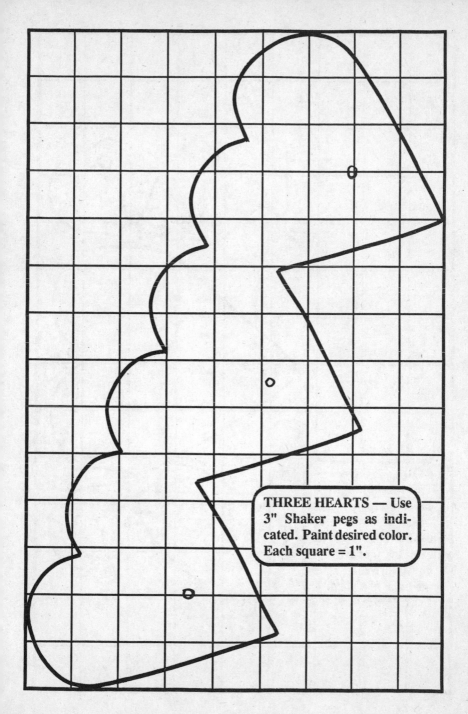

THREE HEARTS — Use 3" Shaker pegs as indicated. Paint desired color. Each square = 1".

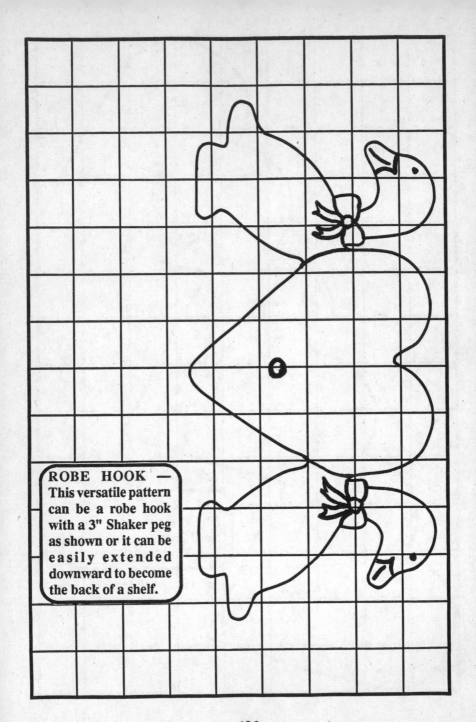

ROBE HOOK —
This versatile pattern can be a robe hook with a 3" Shaker peg as shown or it can be easily extended downward to become the back of a shelf.

MINI-SHELF — Attach brackets to back on lower corners as shown. Attach the shelf as indicated to both the brackets and the back. Rout the outside edges before assembly. Stain or paint as desired. Each square = 1".

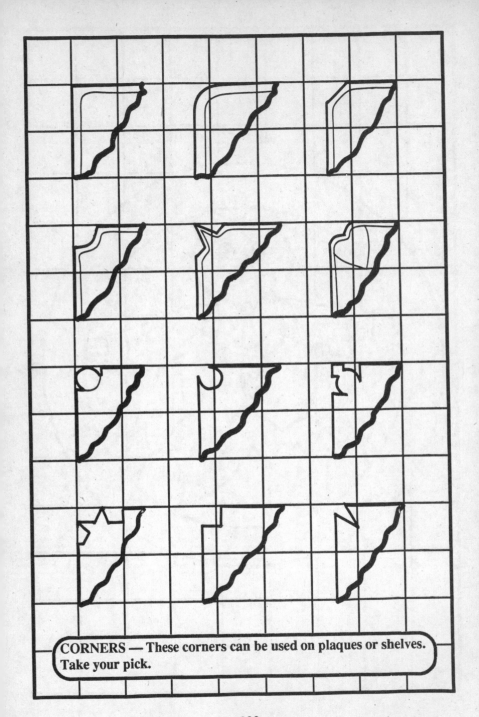

CORNERS — These corners can be used on plaques or shelves. Take your pick.

Refrigerator Magnets

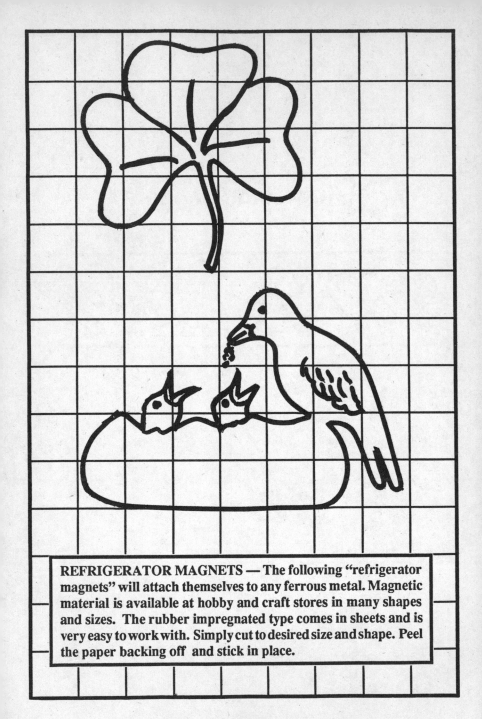

REFRIGERATOR MAGNETS — The following "refrigerator magnets" will attach themselves to any ferrous metal. Magnetic material is available at hobby and craft stores in many shapes and sizes. The rubber impregnated type comes in sheets and is very easy to work with. Simply cut to desired size and shape. Peel the paper backing off and stick in place.

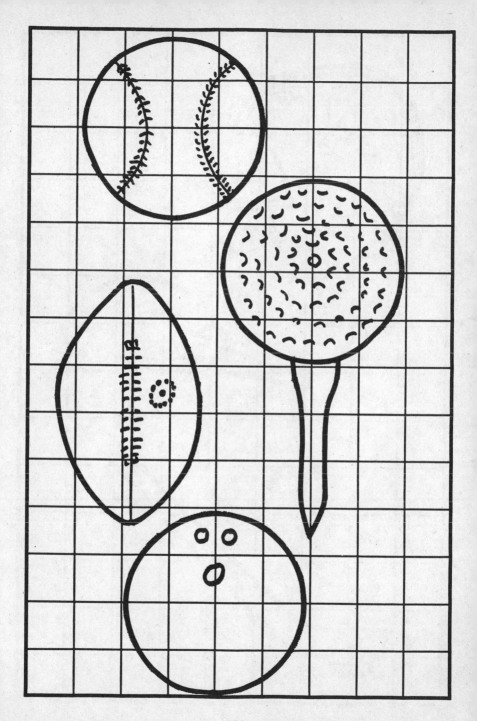

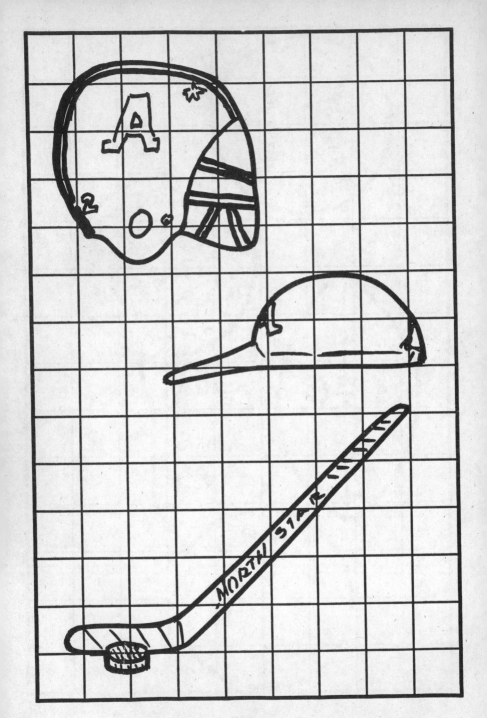

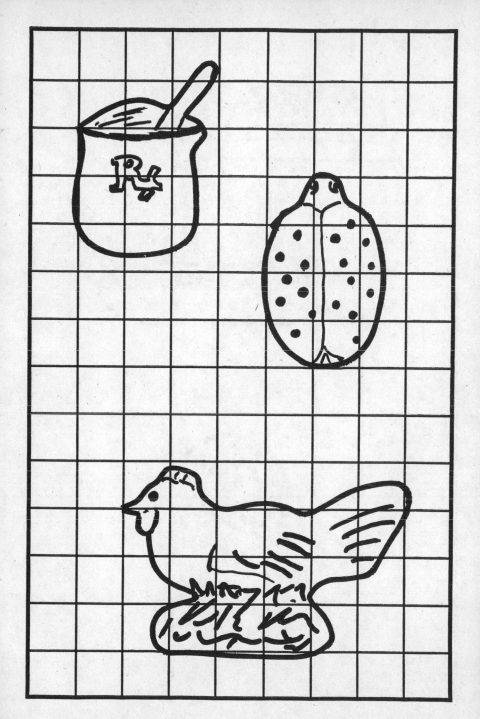

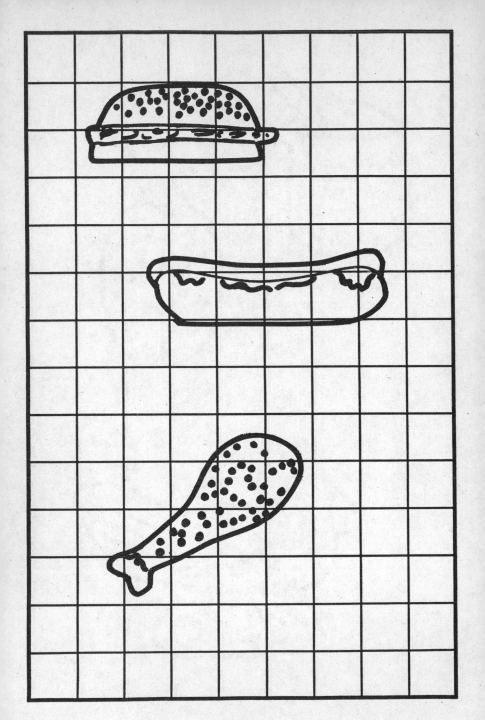

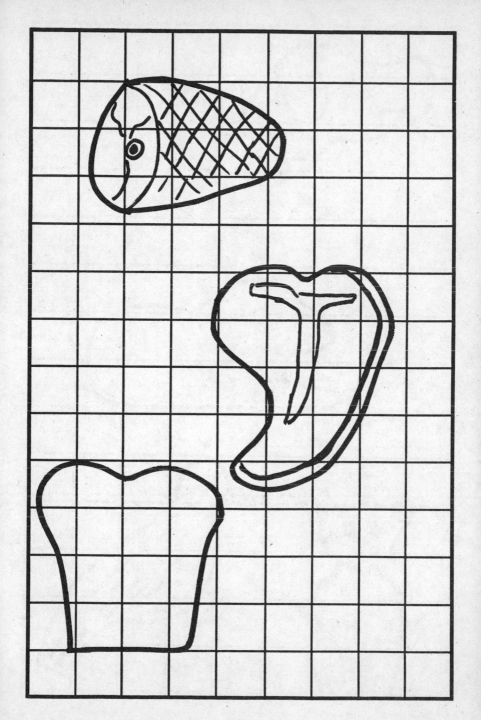

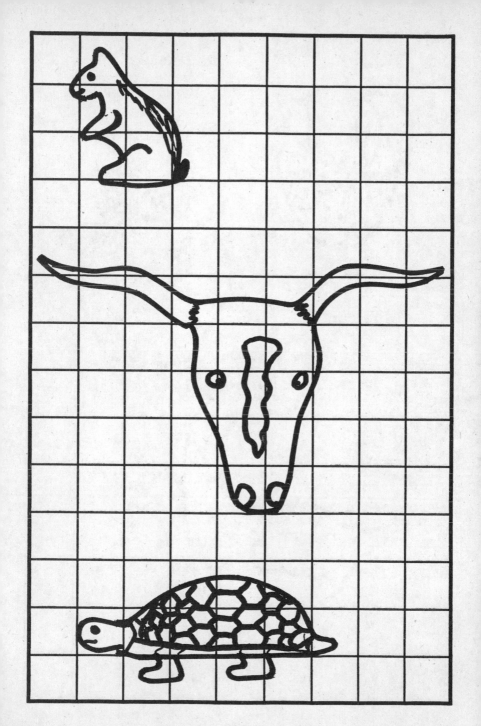

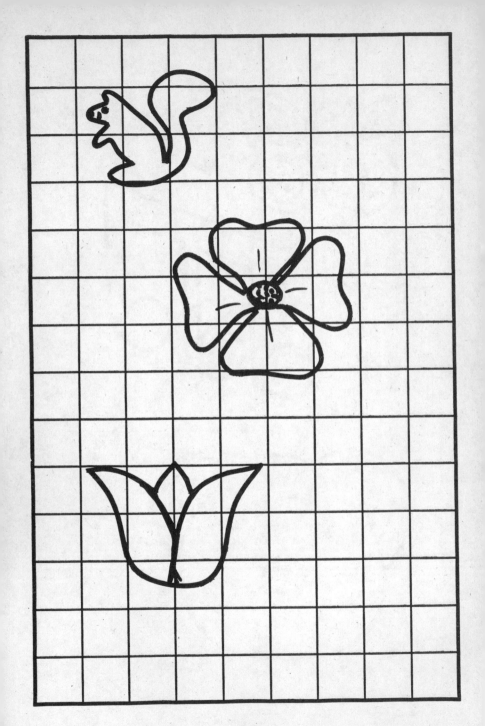

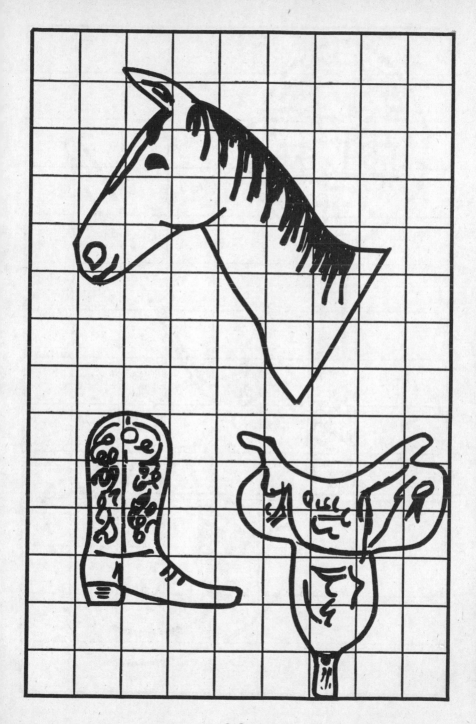

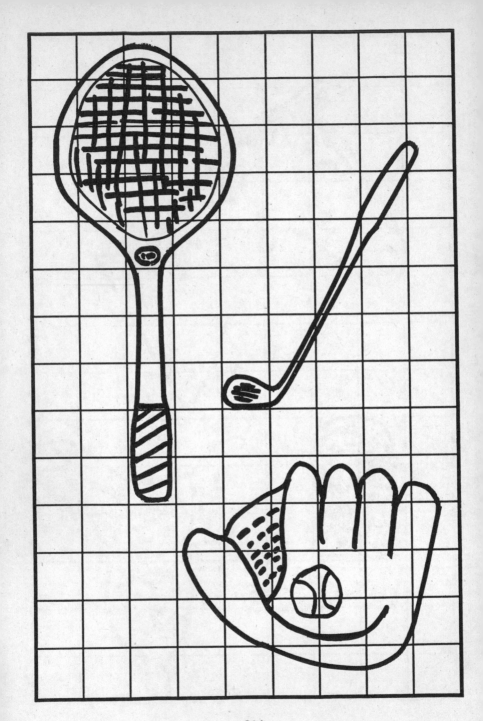

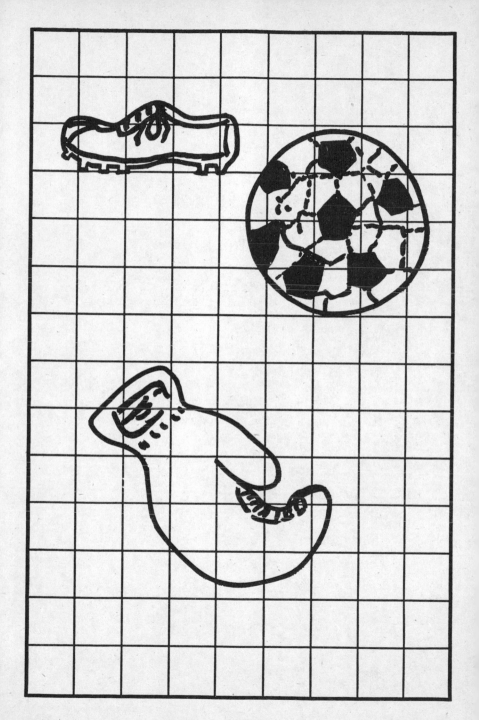

Inside Cuts

INSIDE CUTS — These inside cuts make excellent decorations for shelf tops and supports. They may be attached with any good quality wood glue or small nails.

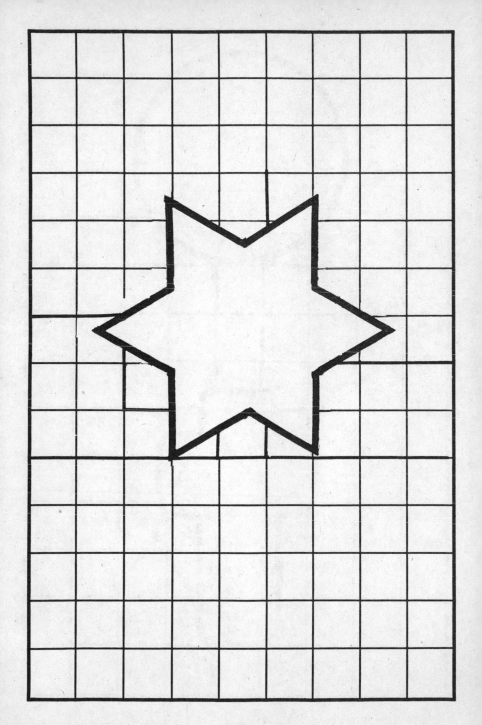

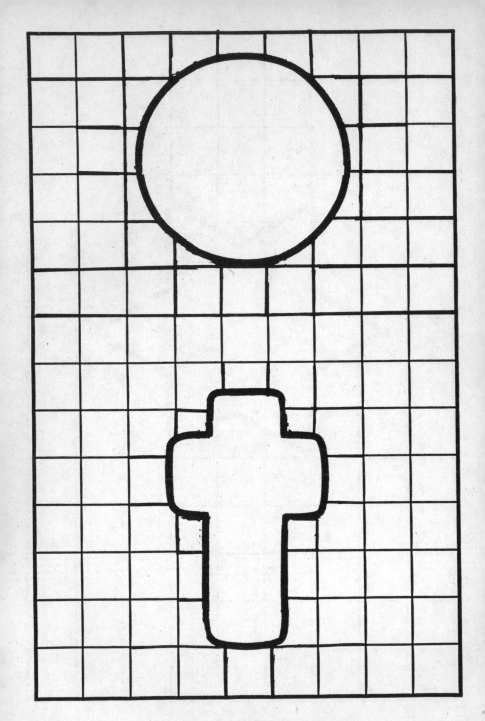

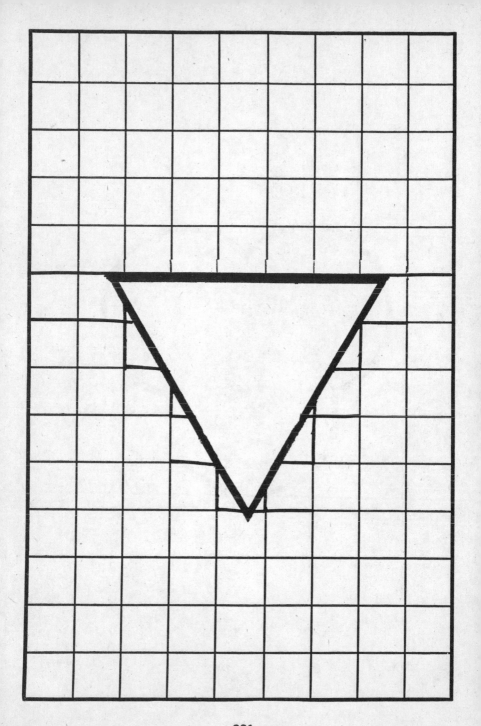

221

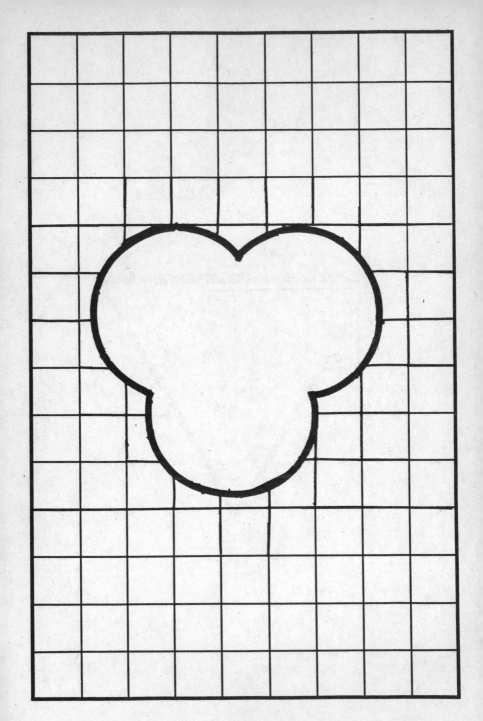

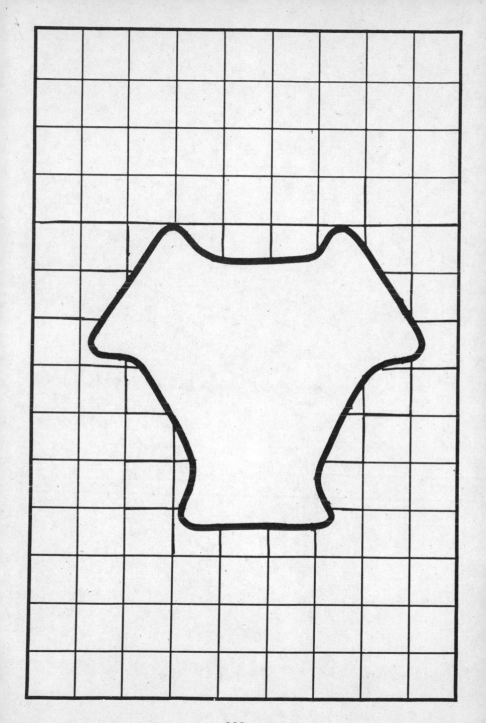

Alphabet and Numerals

ALPHABET AND NUMERALS — These patterns can be used to spell out names for room doors, signs or for plaques. Try decorating the letters with various patterns such as hearts, flowers or geometric shapes for an extra touch.

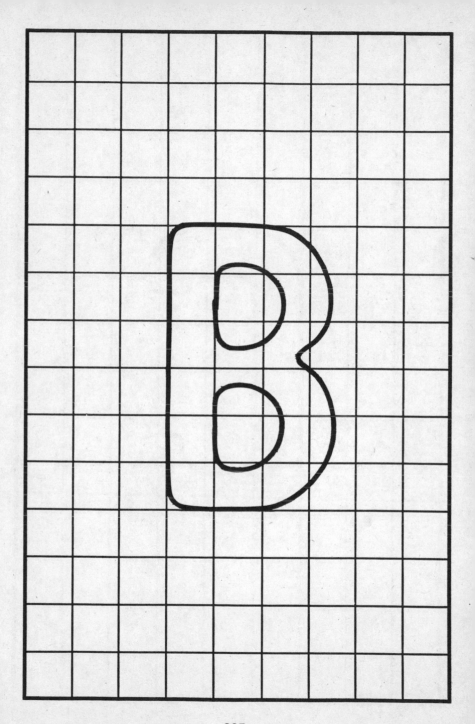

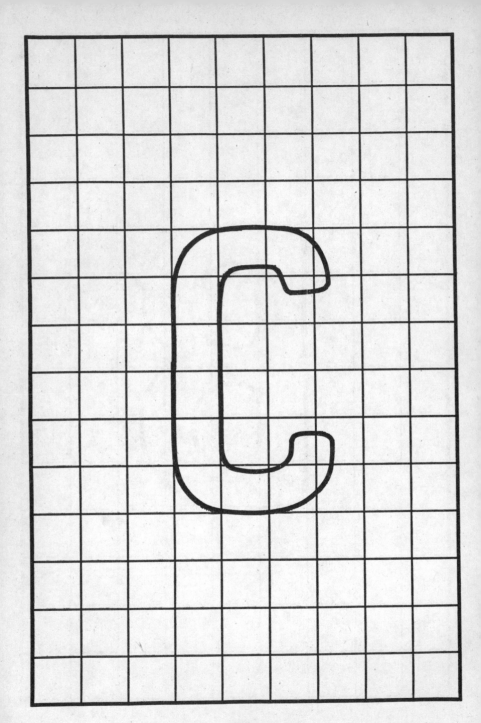

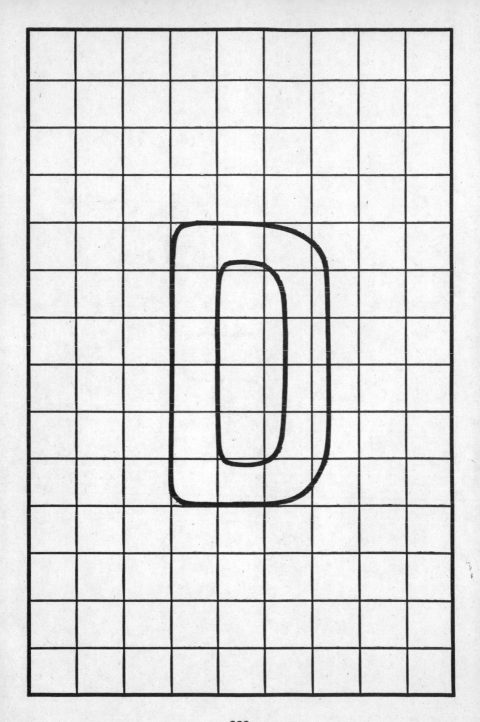

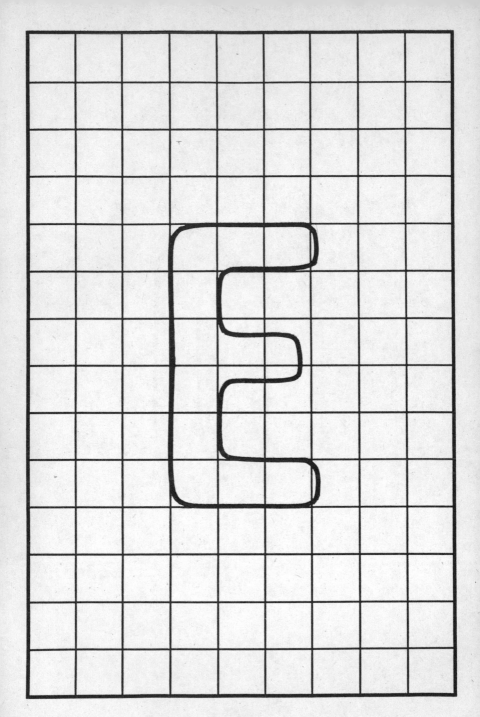

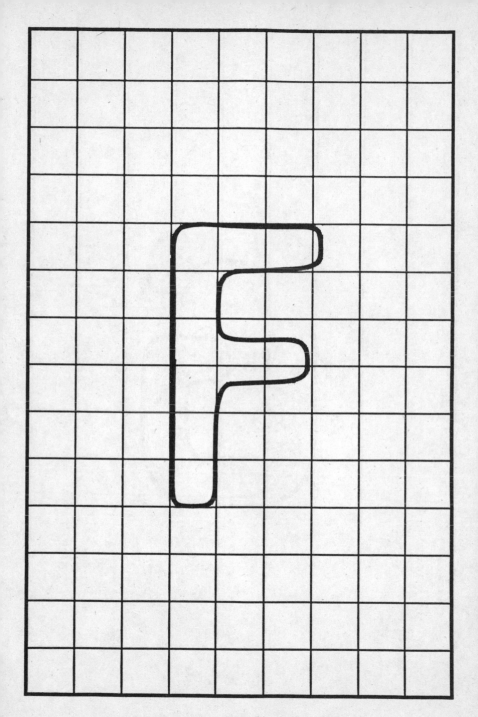

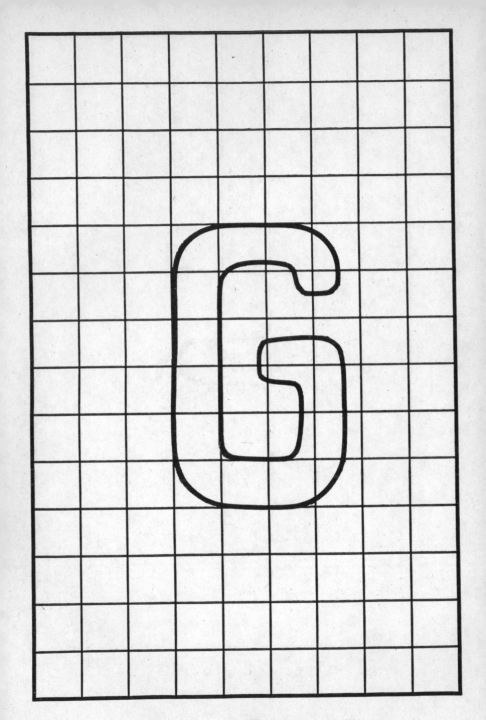

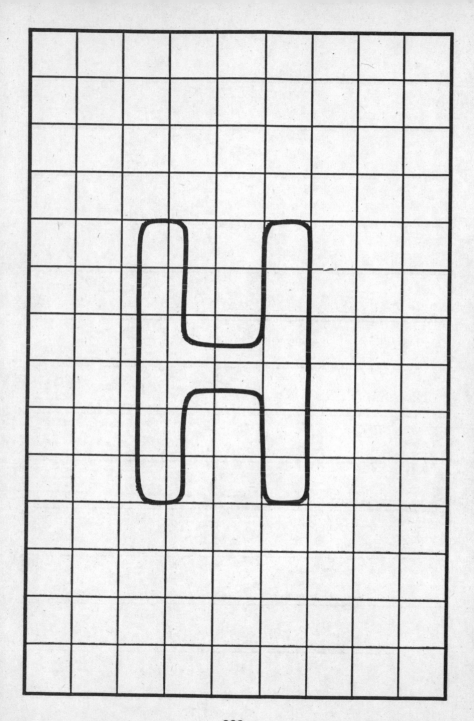

233

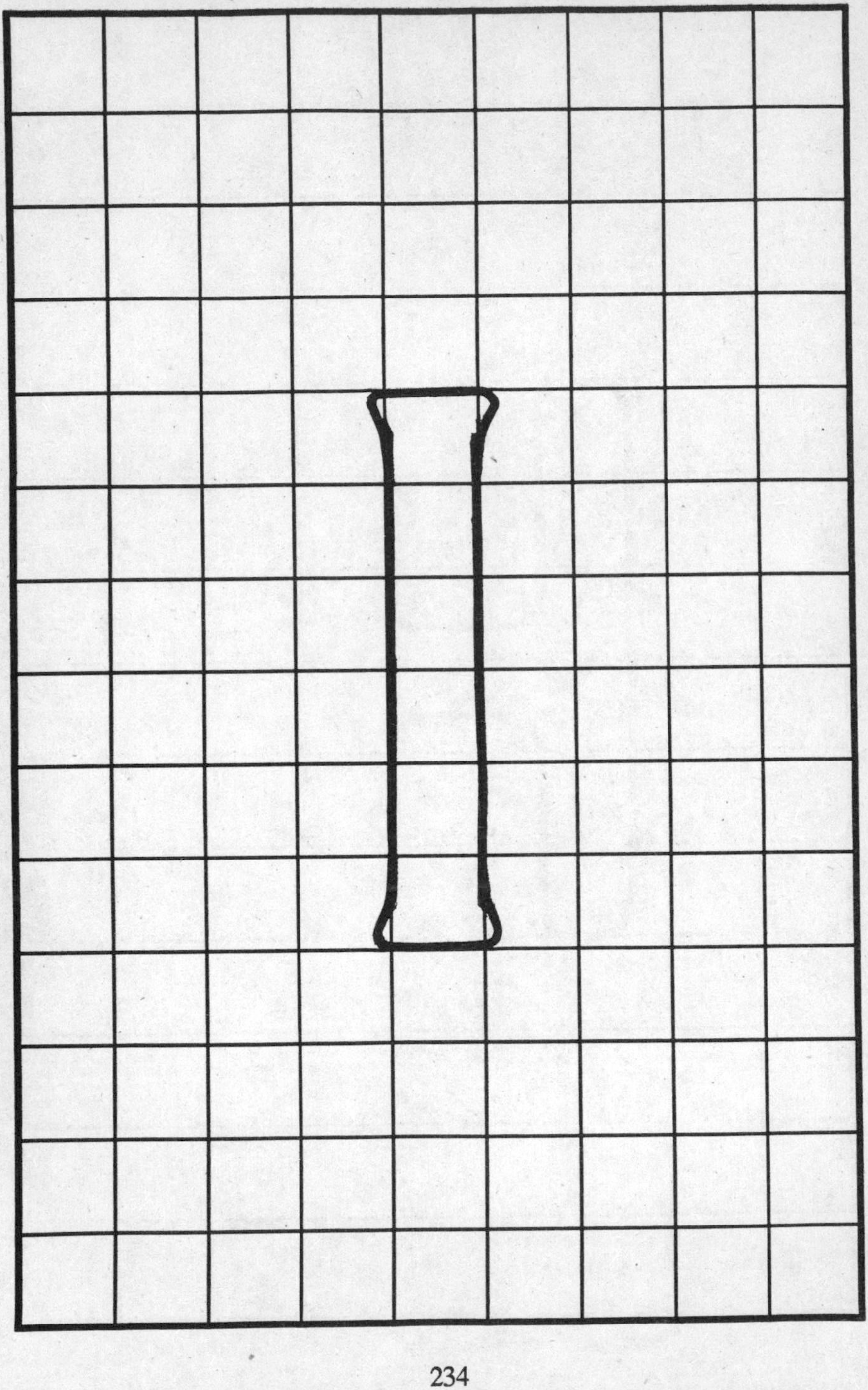

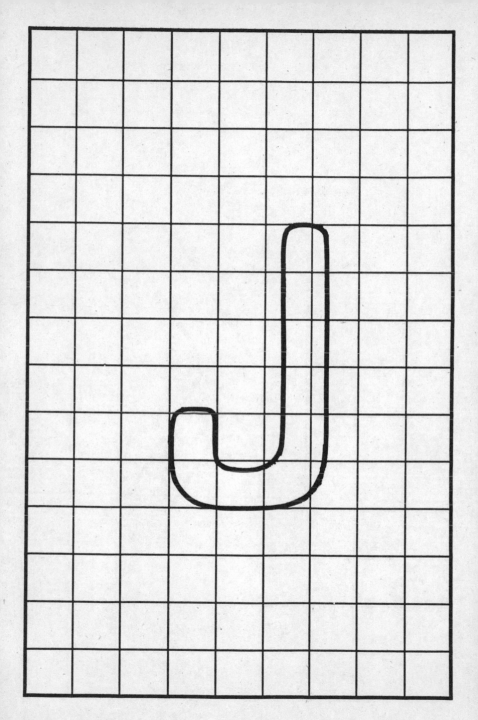

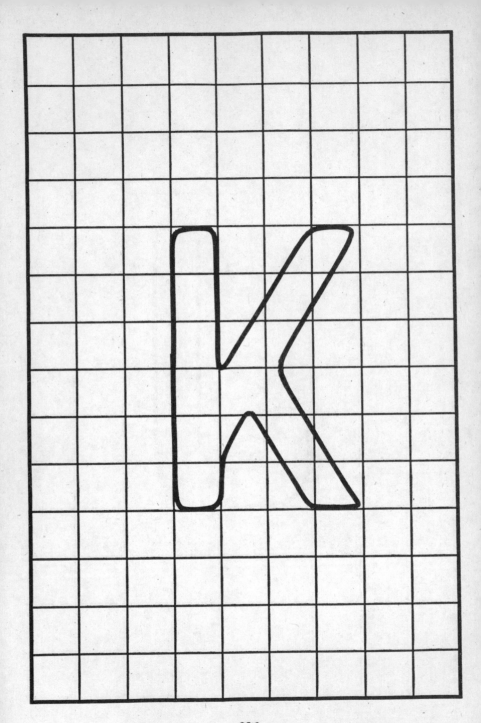

236

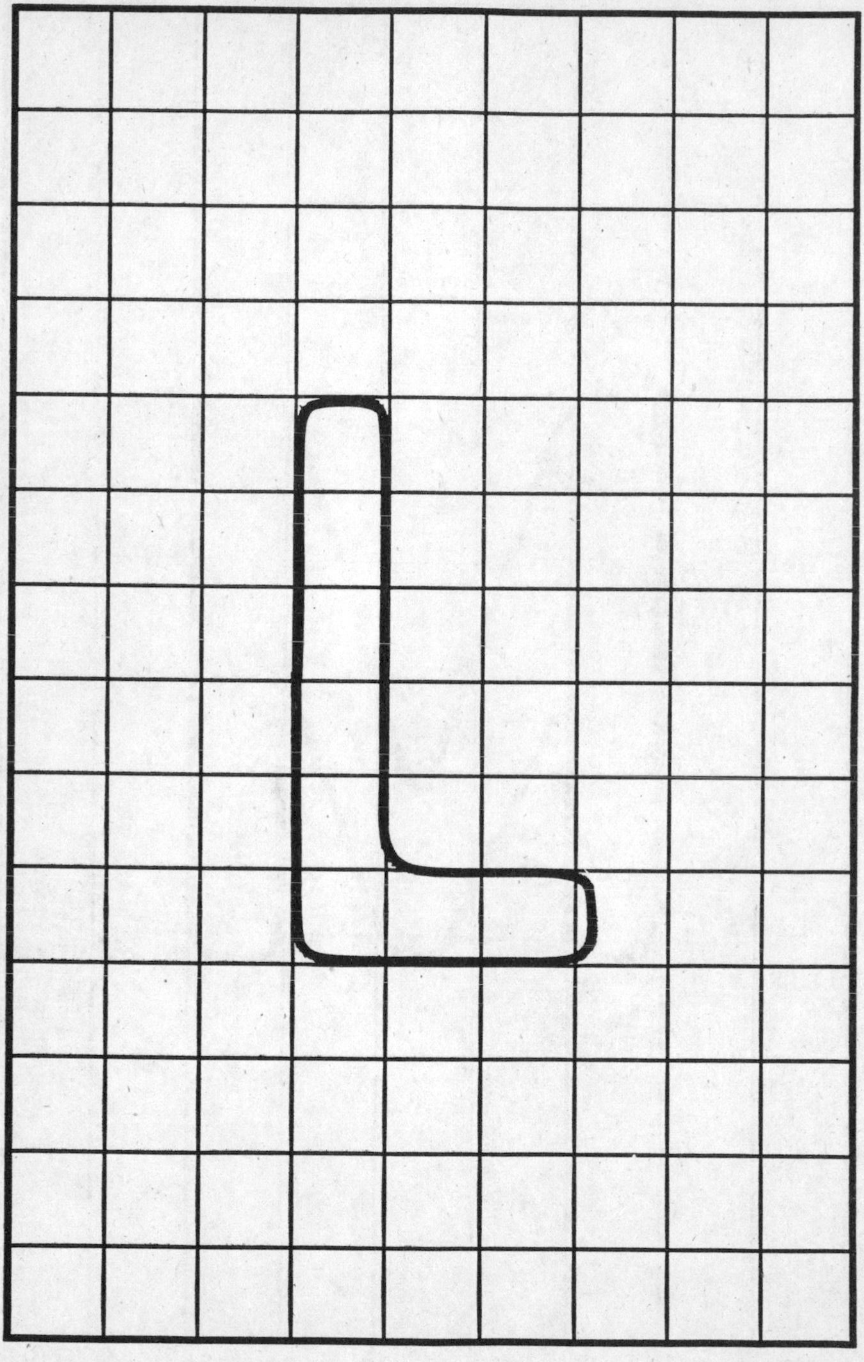

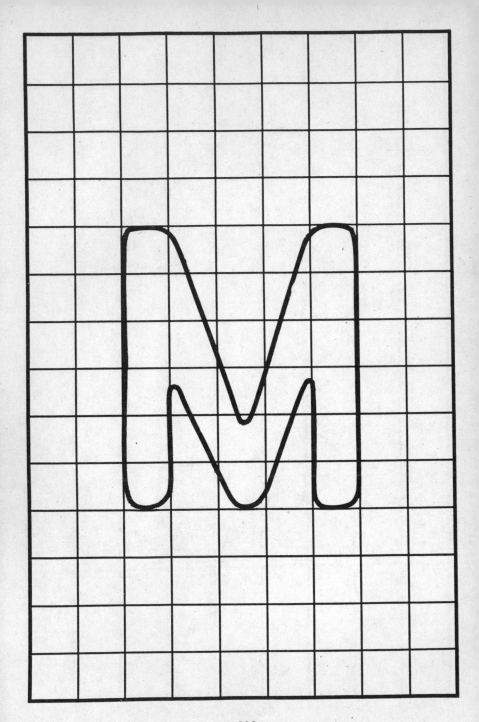

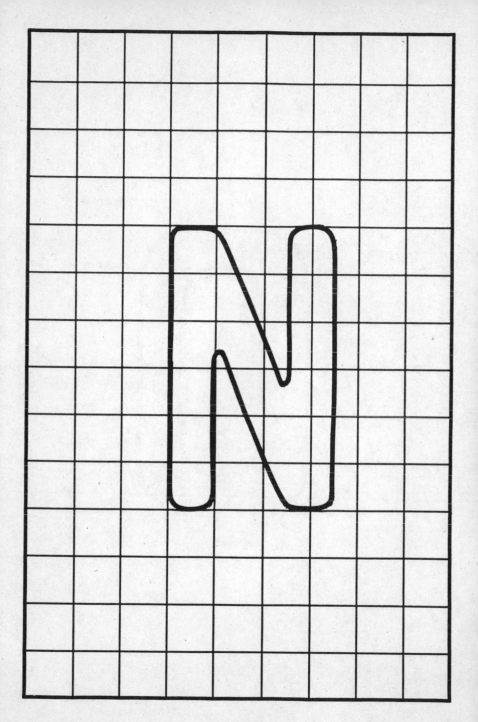

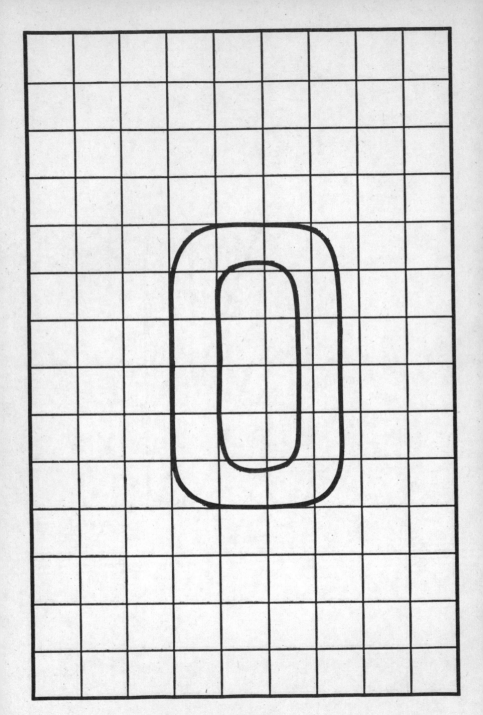

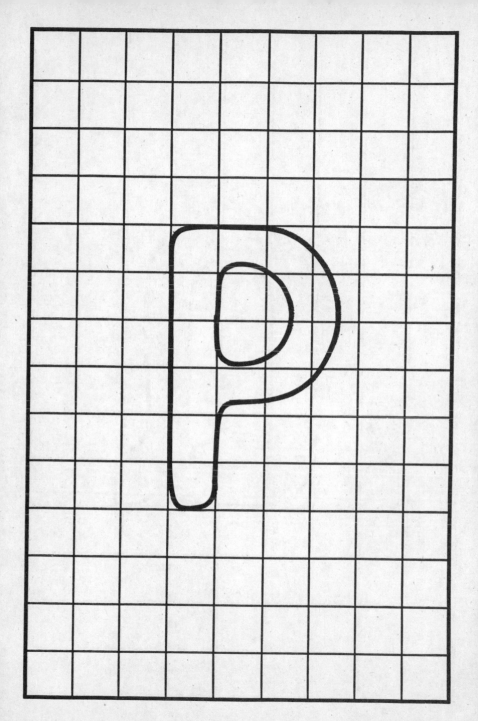

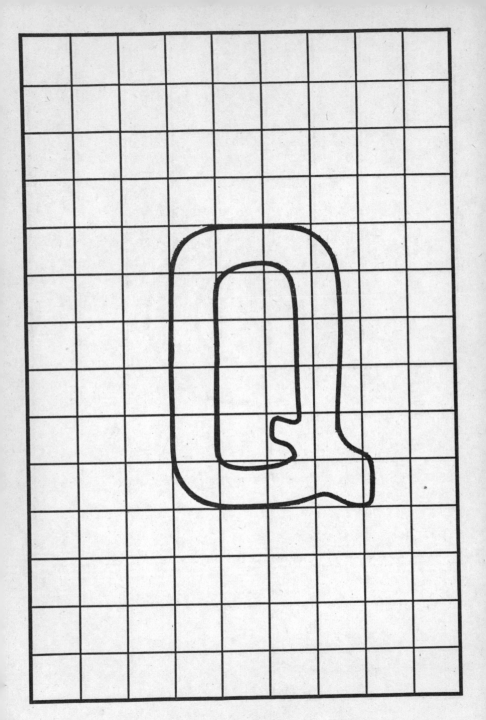

242

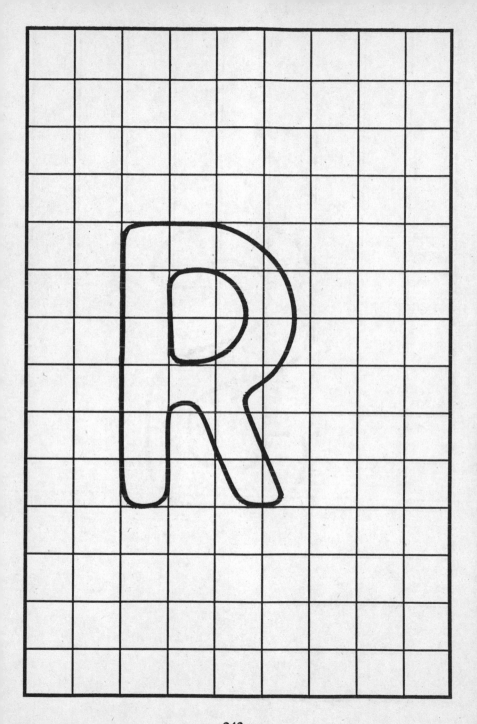

243

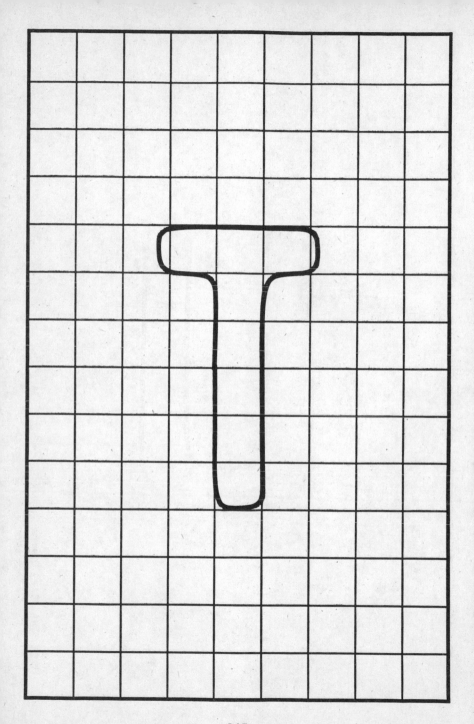

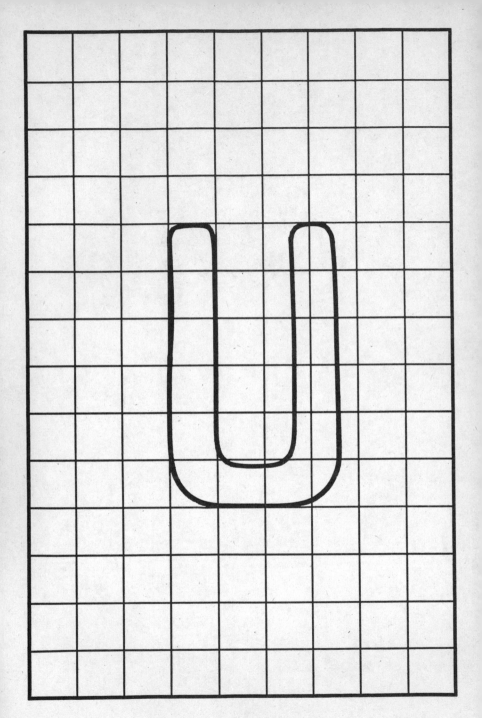

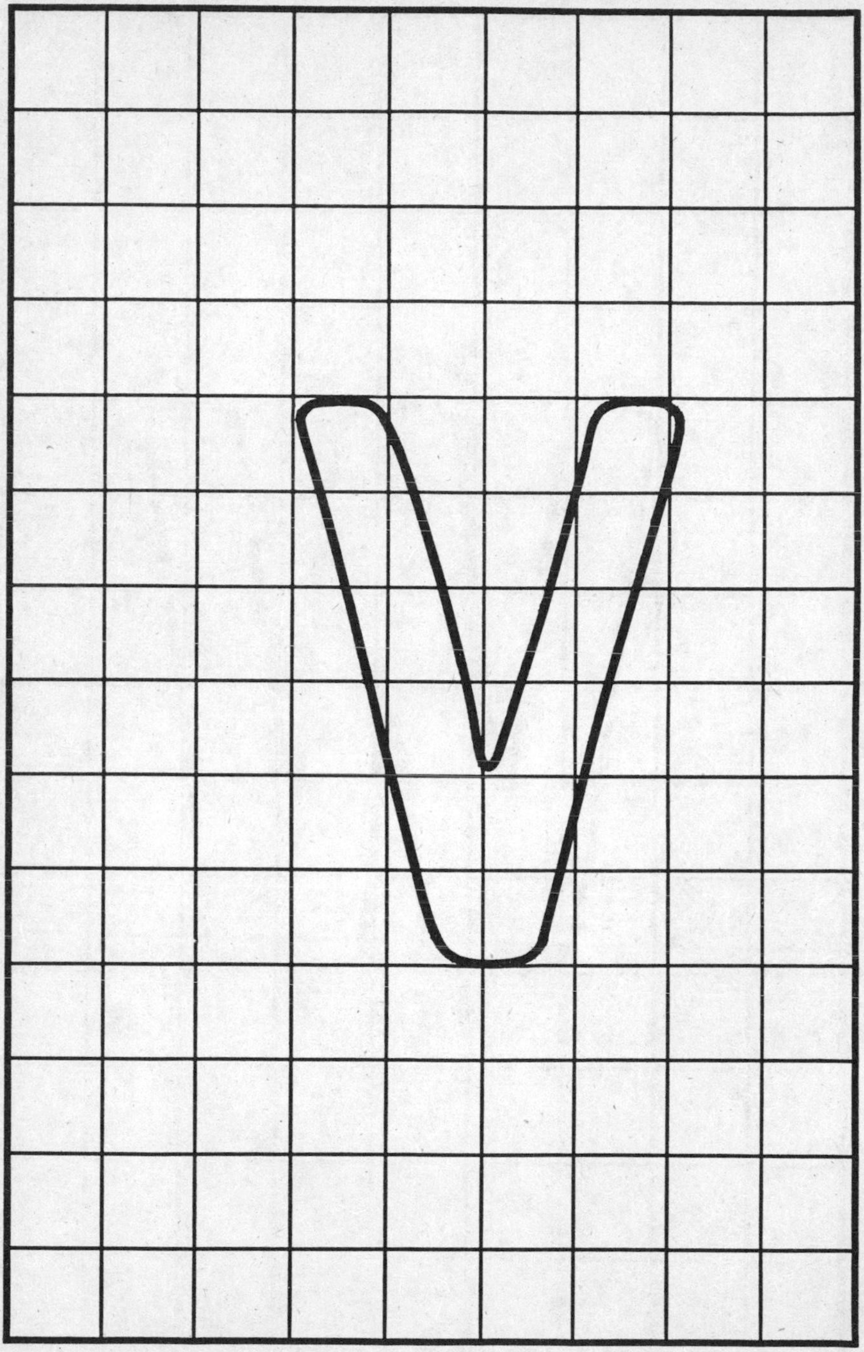

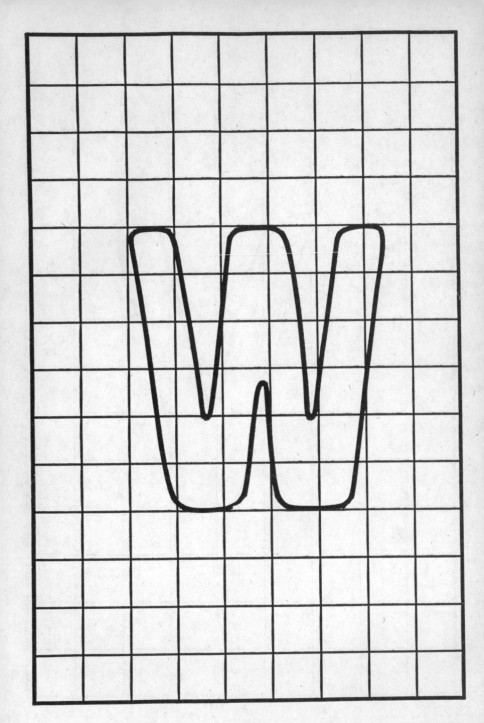

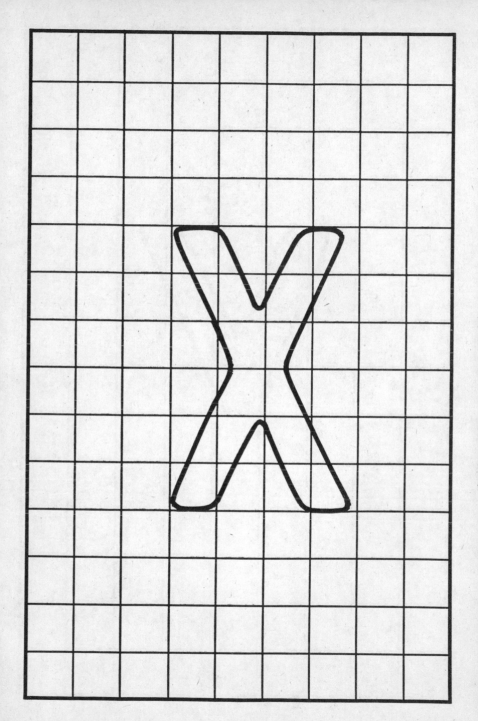

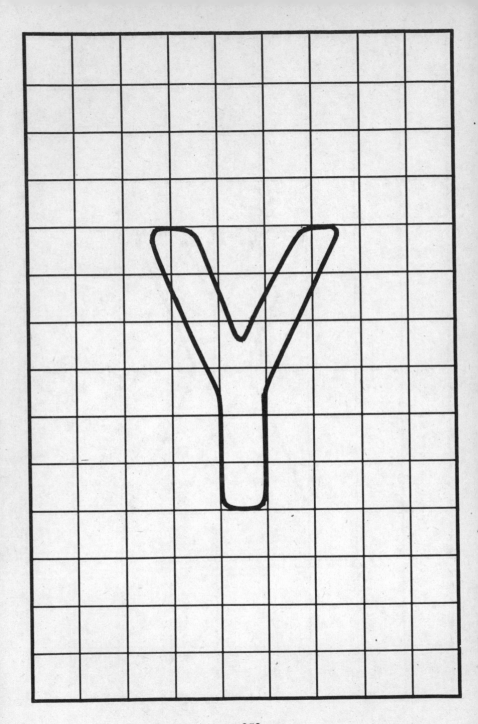

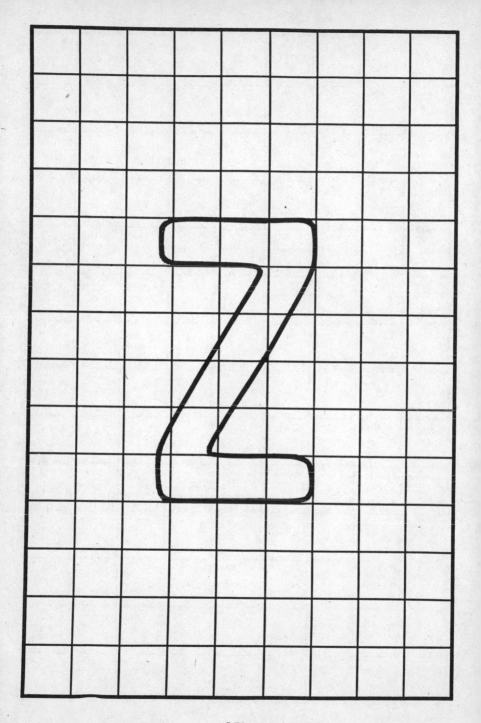

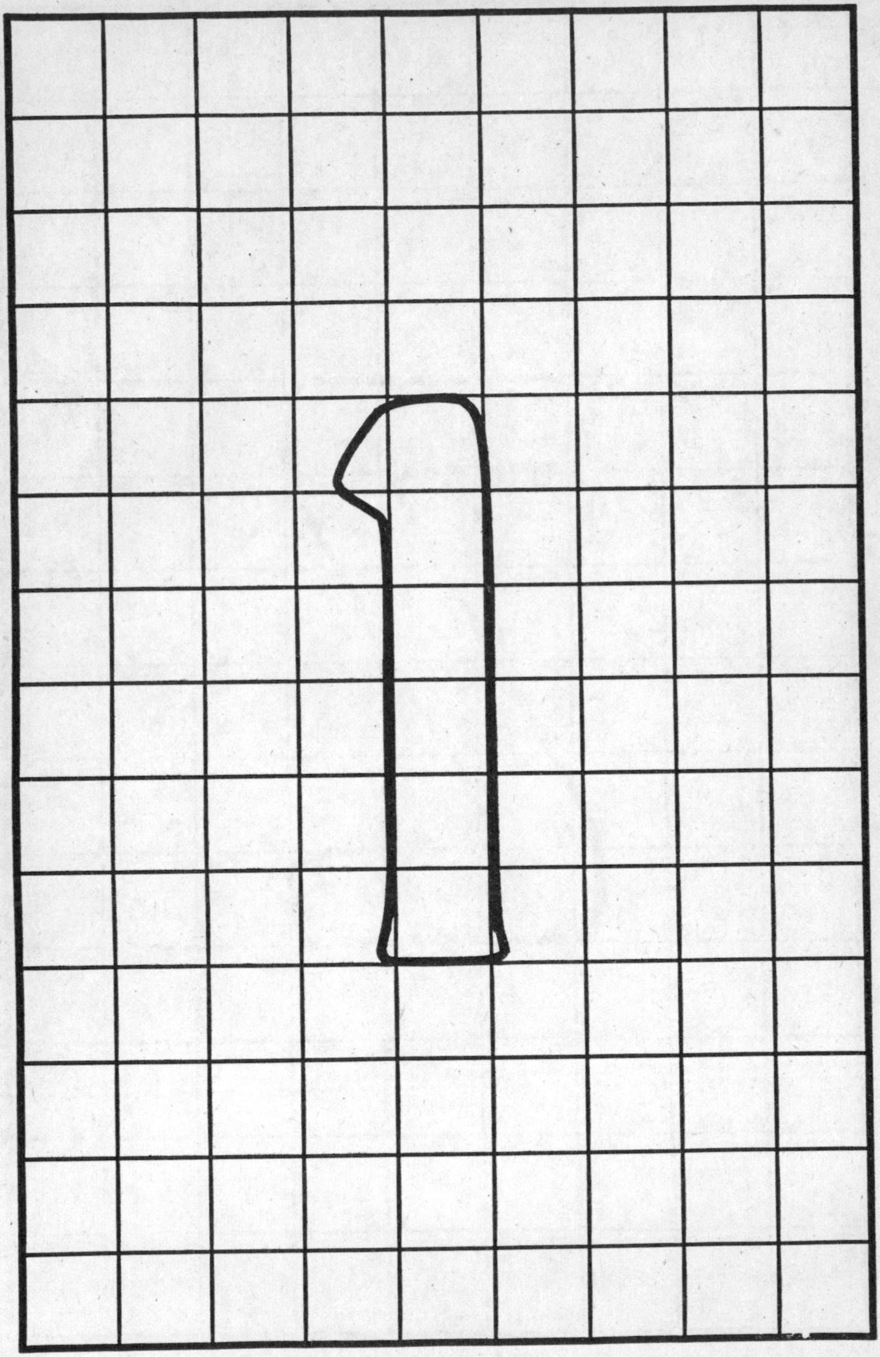

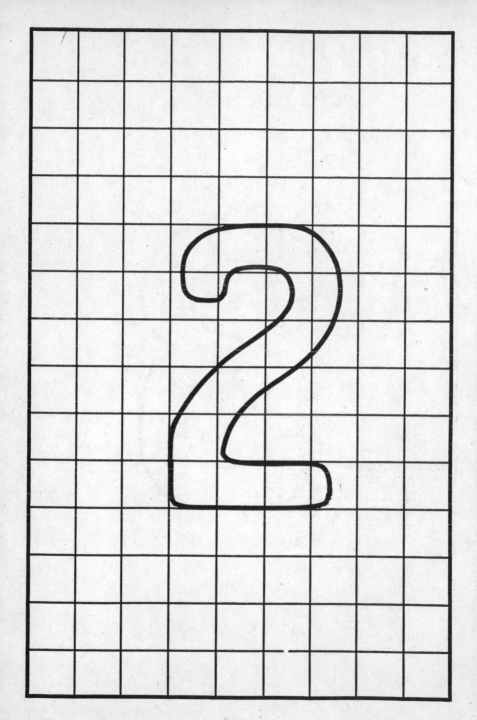

253

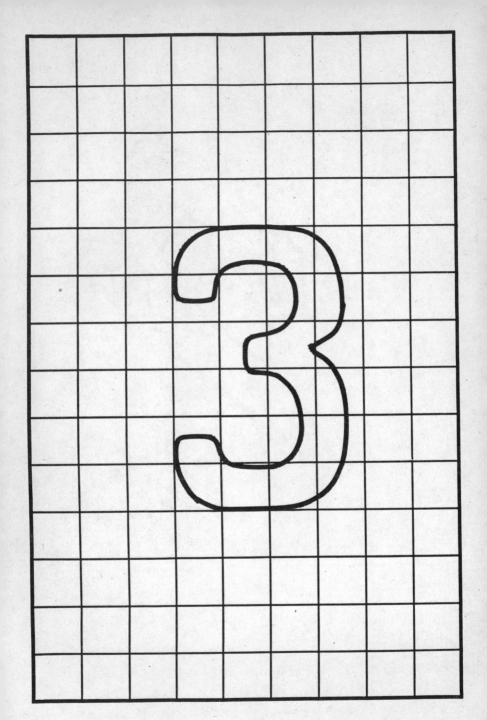

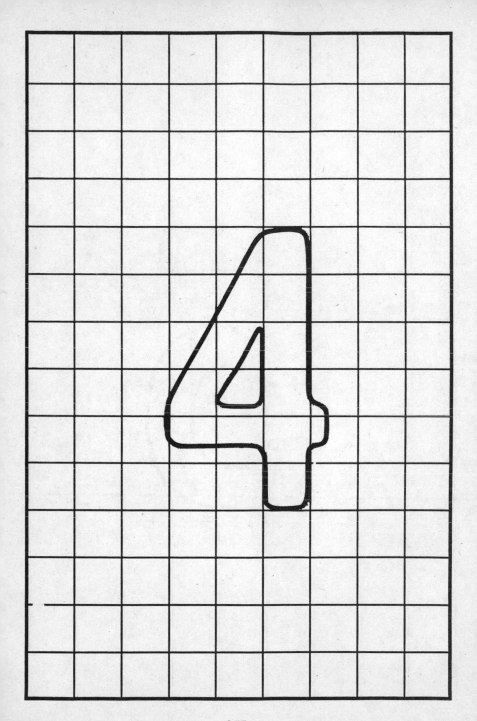

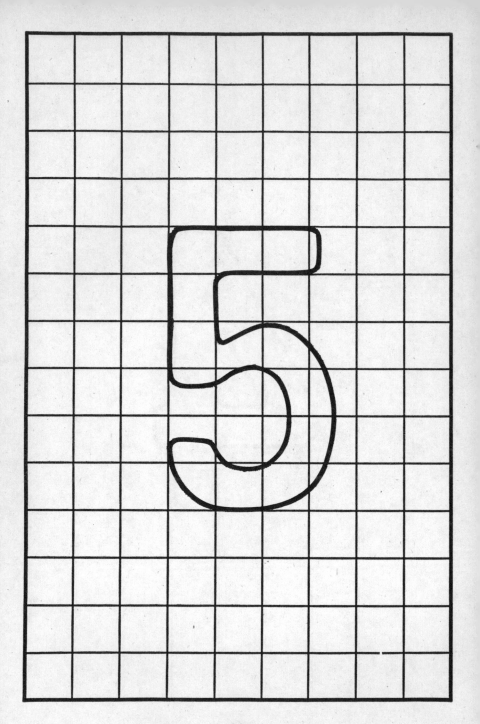

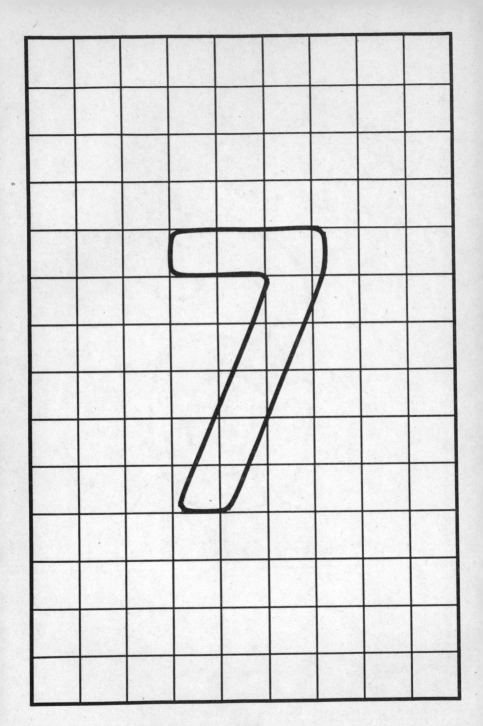

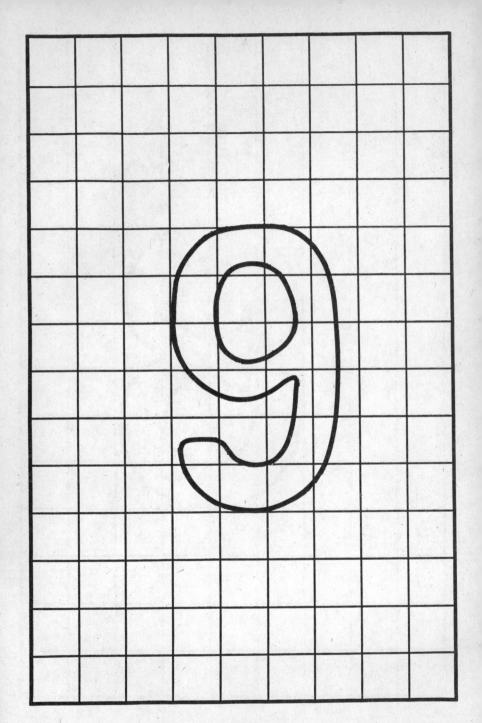

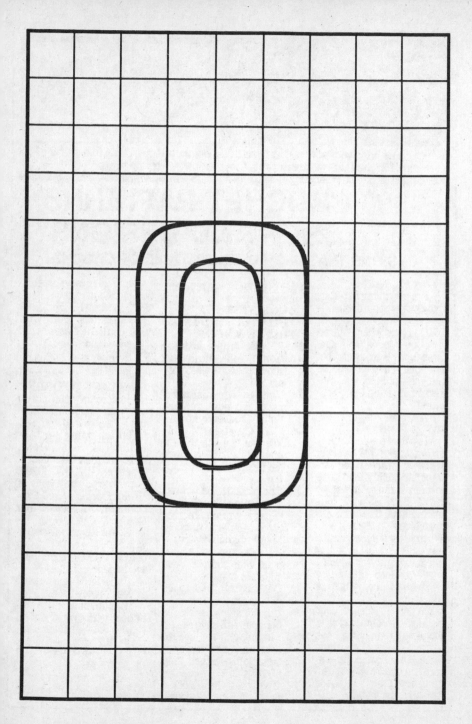

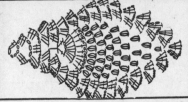